FROM THE NEW WORLD

Also by JORIE GRAHAM

FROM THE NEW WORLD

POEMS 1976–2014

JORIE

GRAHAM

ecco

An Imprint of HarperCollins Publishers

HarperCollins books may be purchased for educational, business, or sales promotional use. For information please e-mail the Special Markets Department at SPsales@harpercollins.com.

FIRST EDITION

Designed by Erica Mena

Library of Congress Cataloging-in-Publication Data has been applied for.

ISBN 978-0-06-231540-3

15   16   17   18   19   INDD/RRD   10   9   8   7   6   5   4   3   2   1

for Peter

ACKNOWLEDGMENTS

Grateful acknowledgment, for the new poems, to the editors of *The London Review of Books, The New Yorker, The Boston Review* and *Lana Turner.*

My thanks to Daniel Halpern, for having believed in the work from the start—at *Antæus* and Ecco, and then at HarperCollins—and for having been my reader, guide, editor, and friend.

To my indispensable designer Erica Mena, and to Sol Kim Bentley—without whose brilliance, tenacity, and generosity of spirit these selected poems would never have made their way to book form—my deep appreciation.

To Alphonse Taghian, Barbara Smith, Beverly Moy, and Jose Baselga, my ongoing gratitude—

and to Emily and Alvaro, my thankfulness for their courage—and to Mark for his friendship—and to Peter for his love.

CONTENTS

from THE ERRANCY

from SWARM

from NEVER

from PLACE

NEW POEMS

from

HYBRIDS OF
PLANTS AND
OF GHOSTS

TENNESSEE JUNE

This is the heat that seeks the flaw in everything
and loves the flaw.
Nothing is heavier than its spirit,
nothing more landlocked than the body within it.
Its daylilies grow overnight, our lawns
bare, then falsely gay, then bare again. Imagine
your mind wandering without its logic,
your body the sides of a riverbed giving in.
In it, no world can survive
having more than its neighbors;
in it, the pressure to become forever less is the pressure
to take forevermore
to get there. Oh

let it touch you.
The porch is sharply lit—little box of the body—
and the hammock swings out easily over its edge.
Beyond, the hot ferns bed, and fireflies gauze
the fat tobacco slums—
the crickets boring holes into the heat the crickets fill.
Rock out into that dark and back to where
the blind moths circle, circle,
back and forth from the bone-white house to the creepers unbraiding.
Nothing will catch you.
Nothing will let you go.
We call it blossoming—
the spirit breaks from you and you remain.

STRANGERS

Indeed the tulips
change tense
too quickly.
They open and fly off.
And, holding absolutes
at bay, the buds

tear through the fruit trees,
steeples into sky.
Faith is where we are
less filled
with ourselves, and are
expected nowhere—

though it's better to hurry.
The starlings keep trying
to thread the eyes
of steeples.
It's hard, you can't
cross over. The skin

of the pear tree is terse
like the pear, and the acorn
knows finally
the road not taken
in the oak.
We have no mind

in a world without objects.
The vigor of our way
is separateness,
the infinite
finding itself strange
among the many. Dusk,

when objects lose their way, you
throw a small
red ball at me
and I return it.
The miracle is this:
the perfect arc

of red we interrupt
over and over
until it is too dark
to see, reaches beyond us
to complete
only itself.

THE GEESE

(Murray, Kentucky, 1977)

Today as I hang out the wash I see them again, a code
as urgent as elegant,
tapering with goals.
For days they have been crossing. We live beneath these geese

as if beneath the passage of time, or a most perfect heading.
Sometimes I fear their relevance.
Closest at hand,
between the lines,

the spiders imitate the paths the geese won't stray from,
imitate them endlessly to no avail:
things will not remain connected,
will not heal,

and the world thickens with texture instead of history,
texture instead of place.
Yet the small fear of the spiders
binds and binds

the pins to the lines, the lines to the eaves, to the pincushion bush,
as if, at any time, things could fall further apart
and nothing could help them
recover their meaning. And if these spiders had their way,

chainlink over the visible world,

would we be in or out? I turn to go back in.

There is a feeling the body gives the mind

of having missed something, a bedrock poverty, like falling

without the sense that you are passing through one world,

that you could reach another

anytime. Instead the real

is crossing you,

your body an arrival

you know is false but can't outrun. And somewhere in between

these geese forever entering and

these spiders turning back,

this astonishing delay, the everyday, takes place.

OVER AND OVER STITCH

Late in the season the world digs in, the fat blossoms
hold still for just a moment longer.
Nothing looks satisfied,
but there is no real reason to move on much further:
this isn't a bad place;
why not pretend

we wished for it?
The bushes have learned to live with their haunches.
The hydrangea is resigned
to its pale and inconclusive utterances.
Towards the end of the season
it is not bad

to have the body. To have experienced joy
as the mere lifting of hunger
is not to have known it
less. The tobacco leaves
don't mind being removed
to the long racks—all uses are astounding

to the used.
There are moments in our lives which, threaded, give us heaven—
noon, for instance, or all the single victories
of gravity, or the kudzu vine,
most delicate of manias,
which has pressed its luck

this far this season.

It shines a gloating green.

Its edges darken with impatience, a kind of wind.

Nothing again will ever be this easy, lives

being snatched up like dropped stitches, the dry stalks of daylilies

marking a stillness we can't keep.

THE WAY THINGS WORK

is by admitting
or opening away.
This is the simplest form
of current: Blue
moving through blue;
blue through purple;
the objects of desire
opening upon themselves
without us;
the objects of faith.
The way things work
is by solution,
resistance lessened or
increased and taken
advantage of.
The way things work
is that we finally believe
they are there,
common and able
to illustrate themselves.
Wheel, kinetic flow,
rising and falling water,
ingots, levers and keys,
I believe in you,
cylinder lock, pulley,
lifting tackle and

crane lift your small head—
I believe in you—
your head is the horizon to
my hand. I believe
forever in the hooks.
The way things work
is that eventually
something catches.

AN ARTICHOKE FOR MONTESQUIEU

Its petals do not open of their own accord. That is our part,
as the whisper is the hand we tender
to the wish, though each
would rather rule the field. What remains
is the heart, its choke a small reminder to be mindful
lest we go too far
for flavor. These are the questions
its petals part in answer to: where
is God? how deep is space? is it inhabited? The artichoke
is here that we imagine
what universe once needed to create it,
penetrable jewel;
what mathematics.
And then, now,

when the earth is no longer the world, it offers
a small believable cosmology:
each tiny leaf an oar
in the battle where each pulled his own; and the whole
the king himself, tiered like his crown or the multitude
laughing. The mind meets the heart
on such terrain as this, where each
can give in to the other
calling it victory,
calling it loss—
a no man's land where each of us
opens, is opened, and where
what we could have done locks to the very core
with what we have.

FRAMING

Something is left out, something left behind. As, for instance,

in this photo of myself at four, the eyes
focus elsewhere, the hand interrupted mid-air by some enormous,
sudden,
fascination.

Something never before seen has happened left of frame,
and everything already known
is more opaque for it.
Beyond the frame is why

the hydrangea midsummer will go no further, though it continues,
why this century, late and turning,
turns away; beyond
is where the story goes after all the knots are tied, and where

the insects meet in order to become
the grand machine they are the perfect parts of; beyond
is what the wind
leans towards, easy as can be, the sheep

we have already counted,
the world too large to fit.
Within, it would have been a mere event,
not destructive as it is now, destructive as the past remains,

becomes, by knowing more than we do.

MIRRORS

For some of us the only way of knowing we are here at all, going
across and going down,
exquisitely temporal though at no point believable; fragile; tragic.
The mirror redeems

the desire to wish,
what we cannot see of ourselves staring back with its most accurate
       face.
The closer you come
the less believable—

life-size that dangerous democracy that will destroy its subjects.
Lookalikes, miniatures,
as in the world of pine, are stabs at freedom:
this limb twisted impossibly, that height not naturally achieved,

achieved. Or,
taking the lodgepole: in the clearings
their maps are unreadable, carrying their off-centeredness
      with vanity,
true love,

slow and doubling like ideas not yet come to term—but stubbornly
growing thick and burying themselves
in themselves
While in the forest,

the modest chemistries of need force all of them to grow cleanly

identical, histories

where only present tense survives,

the lower limbs all shed in compromise—as if in such a crowd

being overlapped and overlooked were being free . . .

Too many arrows

for identical hearts,

unwavering, unvarying, every one a hero, a mind

made up. What industry.

What will we become from lack of uselessness. What will we become

without that acute, fancy love—

branch off my own tree bent back to taunt and almost look alike.

MIND

The slow overture of rain,
each drop breaking
without breaking into
the next, describes
the unrelenting, syncopated
mind. Not unlike
the hummingbirds
imagining their wings
to be their heart, and swallows
believing the horizon
to be a line they lift
and drop. What is it
they cast for? The poplars,
advancing or retreating,
lose their stature
equally, and yet stand firm,
making arrangements
in order to become
imaginary. The city
draws the mind in streets,
and streets compel it
from their intersections
where a little
belongs to no one. It is
what is driven through
all stationary portions
of the world, gravity's

stake in things. The leaves,
pressed against the dank
window of November
soil, remain unwelcome
till transformed, parts
of a puzzle unsolvable
till the edges give a bit
and soften. See how
then the picture becomes clear,
the mind entering the ground
more easily in pieces,
and all the richer for it.

NEW TREES

For long it seemed nothing could be made again of these lean branches,
seamless, eyeless. Who
would have ever known there were so many exits

and that vanity could be regained from any one of them?
In that sleep how the chapters of reason
must have seemed accomplished

like so many brilliantly dissembled butterflies or the flames
mysteriously tucked into the delicate veins of pitch.
Looking at them now, every leaf

waving the others in, there is no way to imagine how
two such maps could ever overlap. And yet
it is what leaves the body after strictest exile there

that we believe in—bigger, so much fuller than the imagined
tree or the kernel of its definition. Tree
in which all that crossed the mind and all that slipped it find

a home and just reward,
in which the present keeps on breaking and is not turned away
by shores because they also break. And where each firm beginning

reaches its precarious destination at the tip,
giddy and unable to ascertain whether, having been attained,
it is instrument

or cause. From such we emerge, ours
a violence done to that stark line drawing *before* strictly to *after*
and from which we break over and over, branching as far

as we can conceive, each image
of ourselves growing increasingly identical like these leaves,
and waving like the mirage waves to keep our eyes from ever letting go.

GIRL AT THE PIANO

It begins, what I can hear, with the train withdrawing from itself
at an even pace in the night although it always seems
to withdraw from us.
Our house almost continues

in its neighbors, although the thinnest bent and wavering fence
keeps us completely strange.
Perhaps it is a daughter who practices the piano, practices
slow and overstressed like the train, slow and relentless

like the crickets weaving their briar between us and growing
    increasingly
unsure of purpose. These three sounds continue, and I
alongside them so that we seem to stand
terribly still. Every change

is into a new childhood, what grows old only the fiber
of remembering, tight at first like crickets and ivories,
crickets and train,
then slackening

though always hanging on to the good bones of windowframes and eaves
and white columns of the porch
in moonlight. Like taffeta, the song,
though not yet learned, is closer to inhabiting her hands

and less her mind, ever closer to believing

it could never have been otherwise. Your sleep beside me is the real,

the loom I can return to when all loosens into speculation.

Silently, the air is woven

by the terribly important shuttle of your breath,

    the air that has crossed

your body retreating, the new air approaching. See,

transformation, or our love of it,

draws a pattern we can't see but own. Like the pennies we pushed

into the soil beneath the pillowy hydrangea, pennies

that will turn the white flowers blue,

or the song I finish past her, the completely learned song

like my other self, a penny slipped next to the heart, a neighbor.

from

EROSION

SAN SEPOLCRO

In this blue light
    I can take you there,
snow having made me
    a world of bone
seen through to. This
    is my house,

my section of Etruscan
    wall, my neighbor's
lemontrees, and, just below
    the lower church,
the airplane factory.
    A rooster

crows all day from mist
    outside the walls.
There's milk on the air,
    ice on the oily
lemonskins. How clean
    the mind is,

holy grave. It is this girl
    by Piero
della Francesca, unbuttoning
    her blue dress,
her mantle of weather,
    to go into

labor. Come, we can go in.
       It is before
the birth of god. No-one
       has risen yet
to the museums, to the assembly
       line—bodies

and wings—to the open air
       market. This is
what the living do: go in.
       It's a long way.
And the dress keeps opening
       from eternity

to privacy, quickening.
       Inside, at the heart,
is tragedy, the present moment
       forever stillborn,
but going in, each breath
       is a button

coming undone, something terribly
       nimble-fingered
finding all of the stops.

READING PLATO

This is the story
    of a beautiful
lie, what slips
    through my fingers,
your fingers. It's winter,
    it's far

in the lifespan
    of man.
Bareheaded, in a soiled
    shirt,
speechless, my friend
    is making

lures, his hobby. Flies
    so small
he works with tweezers and
    a magnifying glass.
They must be
    so believable

they're true—feelers,
    antennae,
quick and frantic
    as something
drowning. His heart
    beats wildly

in his hands. It is
    blinding
and who will forgive him
    in his tiny
garden? He makes them
    out of hair,

deer hair, because it's hollow
    and floats.
Past death, past sight,
    this is
his good idea, what drives
    the silly days

together. Better than memory. Better
    than love.
Then they are done, a hook
    under each pair
of wings, and it's Spring,
    and the men

wade out into the riverbed
    at dawn. Above,
the stars still connect-up
    their hungry animals.
Soon they'll be satisfied
    and go. Meanwhile

upriver, downriver, imagine, quick
    in the air,
in flesh, in a blue
    swarm of
flies, our knowledge of
    the graceful

deer skips easily across
  the surface.
Dismembered, remembered,
  it's finally
alive. Imagine
  the body

they were all once
  a part of,
these men along the lush
  green banks
trying to slip in
  and pass

for the natural world.

SCIROCCO

In Rome, at 26
        Piazza di Spagna,
at the foot of a long
        flight of
stairs, are rooms
        let to Keats

in 1820,
        where he died. Now
you can visit them,
        the tiny terrace,
the bedroom. The scraps
        of paper

on which he wrote
        lines
are kept behind glass,
        some yellowing,
some xeroxed or
        mimeographed. . . .

Outside his window
        you can hear the scirocco
working
        the invisible.
Every dry leaf of ivy
        is fingered,

refingered. Who is
        the nervous spirit
of this world
        that must go over and over
what it already knows,
        what is it

so hot and dry
        that's looking through us,
by us,
        for its answer?
In the arbor
        on the terrace

the stark hellenic
        forms
of grapes have appeared.
        They'll soften
till weak enough
        to enter

our world, translating
        helplessly
from the beautiful
        to the true. . . .
Whatever the spirit,
        the thickening grapes

are part of its looking,
        and the slow hands
that made this mask
        of Keats
in his other life,
        and the old woman,

the memorial's
		custodian,
sitting on the porch
		beneath the arbor
sorting chick-peas
		from pebbles

into her cast-iron
		pot.
See what her hands
		know—
they are its breath,
		its mother

tongue, dividing,
		discarding.
There is light playing
		over the leaves,
over her face,
		making her

abstract, making
		her quick
and strange. But she
		has no care
for what speckles her,
		changing her,

she is at
		her work. Oh how we want
to be taken
		and changed,
want to be mended
		by what we enter.

Is it thus
            with the world?
Does it wish us
            to mend it,
light and dark,
            green

and flesh? Will it
            be free then?
I think the world
            is a desperate
element. It would have us
            calm it,

receive it. Therefore this
            is what I
must ask you
            to imagine: wind;
the moment
            when the wind

drops; and grapes,
            which are nothing,
which break
            in your hands.

I WATCHED A SNAKE

hard at work in the dry grass
    behind the house
catching flies. It kept on
    disappearing.
And though I know this has
    something to do

with lust, today it seemed
    to have to do
with work. It took it almost half
    an hour to thread
roughly ten feet of lawn,
    so slow

between the blades you couldn't see
    it move. I'd watch
its path of body in the grass go
    suddenly invisible
only to reappear a little
    further on

black knothead up, eyes on
    a butterfly.
This must be perfect progress where
    movement appears
to be a vanishing, a mending
    of the visible

by the invisible—just as we
    stitch the earth,
it seems to me, each time
    we die, going
back under, coming back up. . . .
    It is the simplest

stitch, this going where we must,
    leaving a not
unpretty pattern by default. But going
    out of hunger
for small things—flies, words—going
    because one's body

goes. And in this disconcerting creature
    a tiny hunger,
one that won't even press
    the dandelions down,
retrieves the necessary blue-
    black dragonfly

that has just landed on a pod . . .
    all this to say
I'm not afraid of them
    today, or anymore
I think. We are not, were not, ever
    wrong. Desire

is the honest work of the body,
    its engine, its wind.
It too must have its sails—wings
    in this tiny mouth, valves

in the human heart, meanings like sailboats
    setting out

over the mind. Passion is work
    that retrieves us,
lost stitches. It makes a pattern of us,
    it fastens us
to sturdier stuff
    no doubt.

WANTING A CHILD

How hard it is for the river here to re-enter

the sea, though it's most beautiful, of course, in the waste

of time where it's almost

turned back. Then

it's yoked,

trussed. . . . The river

has been everywhere, imagine, dividing, discerning,

cutting deep into the parent rock,

scouring and scouring

its own bed.

Nothing is whole

where it has been. Nothing

remains unsaid.

sometimes I'll come this far from home

merely to dip my fingers in this glittering, archaic

sea that renders everything

identical, flesh

where mind and body

blur. The seagulls squeak, ill-fitting

hinges, the beach is thick

with shells. The tide

is always pulsing upward, inland, into the river's rapid

argument, pushing

with its insistent tragic waves—the living echo,

says my book, of some great storm far out at sea, too far

to be recalled by us

but transferred

whole onto this shore by waves, so that erosion

is its very face.

MY GARDEN, MY DAYLIGHT

My neighbor brings me bottom fish—
    tomcod, rockcod—
a fist of ocean. He comes out
    from the appletrees between us
holding his gift like a tight
    spool of thread.

Once a week he brings me fresh-catch,
    boned and skinned
and rolled up like a tongue. I freeze them,
    speechless, angelic
instruments. I have a choir of them.
    Alive, they feed

driving their bodies through the mud,
    mud through their flesh.
See how white they become. High above,
    the water thins
to blue, then air, then less. . . .
    These aren't as sweet

as those that shine up there,
    quick schools
forever trying to slur over, become water.
    But these belong to us
who cannot fall out of this world
    but only deeper

into it, driving it into the white
    of our eyes. Muddy
daylight, we utter it, we drown in it.
    You can stay dry
if you can step between the raindrops
    mother's mother

said. She's words now you can't hear.
    I try to wind my way
between what's here: chalk, lily, milk,
    titanium, snow—
as far as I can say
    these appleblossoms house

five shades of white, and yet
    I know there's more.
Between my held breath and its small hot
    death, a garden,
whiteness, grows. Its icy fruit
    seems true,

it glows. *For free* he says
    so that I can't refuse.

SALMON

I watched them once, at dusk, on television, run,
in our motel room half-way through
Nebraska, quick, glittering, past beauty, past
the importance of beauty,
archaic,
not even hungry, not even endangered, driving deeper and deeper
into less. They leapt up falls, ladders,
and rock, tearing and leaping, a gold river
and a blue river traveling
in opposite directions.
They would not stop, resolution of will
and helplessness, as the eye
is helpless
when the image forms itself, upside-down, backward,
driving up into
the mind, and the world
unfastens itself
from the deep ocean of the given. . . . Justice, aspen
leaves, mother attempting
suicide, the white night-flying moth
the ants dismantled bit by bit and carried in
right through the crack
in my wall. . . . How helpless
the still pool is,
upstream,
awaiting the gold blade
of their hurry. Once, indoors, a child,

I watched, at noon, through slatted wooden blinds,

a man and woman, naked, eyes closed,

climb onto each other,

on the terrace floor,

and ride—two gold currents

wrapping round and round each other, fastening,

unfastening. I hardly knew

what I saw. Whatever shadow there was in that world

it was the one each cast

onto the other,

the thin black seam

they seemed to be trying to work away

between them. I held my breath.

As far as I could tell, the work they did

with sweat and light

was good. I'd say

they traveled far in opposite

directions. What is the light

at the end of the day, deep, reddish-gold, bathing the walls,

the corridors, light that is no longer light, no longer clarifies,

illuminates, antique, freed from the body of

the air that carries it. What is it

for the space of time

where it is useless, merely

beautiful? When they were done, they made a distance

one from the other

and slept, outstretched,

on the warm tile

of the terrace floor,

smiling, faces pressed against the stone.

OF UNEVENNESS

this is our god, the Summer
    Solstice, yearly
buried, resurrected, the longest
    day. And what am I
to do with it, this fingerswidth
    of extra light

I am about to lose? What plant in it
    would grow? I'm on
my porch and staring into it. The jay
    that lives here
threads an extra fly or two tonight,
    no doubt. . . . The real

is a nation of such inroads—the jay
    on Indigo, the note he calls
on what I hear, inroads
    of being found
on being lost. Tomorrow
    this gift

will have gone under once again,
    and for a year
these hundred twenty seconds be
    the hinge, the buried
quick, what throws the rest of each day
    off enough

to make it run. The quick given the jay
    is glut
of blue, and to the rose the extra
    given is the bloom,
the wading out into delay. And to
    the mind

this almost wholly lifting hem
    is given.
And though I can't see any more
    today
than yesterday, it's true, I can
    push out

and take root in that tiny space
    which is as far,
precisely, as the visible will ever go,
    while the progressive
loss of light from here on in
    is runner, stem,

and, in the darkest instance, blossom to
    this narrow tract,
this buried, infinite precision,
    this heaven. . . .

MASACCIO'S EXPULSION

Is this really the failure
    of silence,
or eternity, where these two
    suffer entrance
into the picture
    plane,

a man and woman
    so hollowed
by grief they cover
    their eyes
in order not to see
    the inexhaustible grammar

before them—labor, judgment,
    saints and peddlers—
the daylight hopelessly even
    upon them,
and our eyes, But this too
    is a garden

I'd say, with its architecture
    of grief,
its dark and light
    in the folds
of clothing, and oranges
    for sale

among the shadows
      of oranges, All round them,
on the way down
      toward us,
woods thicken. And perhaps
      it is a flaw

on the wall of this church, or age,
      or merely the restlessness
of the brilliant
      young painter,
the large blue bird
      seen flying too low

just where the trees
      clot. I
want to say to them
      who have crossed
into this terrifying
      usefulness—symbols,

balancing shapes in
      a composition,
mother and father,
      hired hands—
I want to say to them,
      Take your faces

out of your hands,
      look at that bird,
the gift of
      the paint—
I've seen it often
      here

in my life,

    a Sharp-Shinned Hawk,

tearing into the woods

    for which it's

too big, abandoning

    the open

prairie in which

    it is free and easily

eloquent. Watch

    where it will not

veer but follows

    the stain

of woods,

    a long blue arc

breaking itself

    through the wet

black ribs

    of those trees,

seeking a narrower

    place. Always

I find the feathers

    afterward. . . .

Perhaps you know

    why it turns in

this way

    and will not stop?

In the foreground

    almost life-size

the saints hawk their wares,

    and the women,

and merchants. They too
    are traveling
a space too small
    to fit in,
calling out names
    or prices

or proof of faith.
    Whatever they are,
it beats
    up through the woods
of their bodies,
    almost a light, up

through their fingertips,
    their eyes.
There isn't a price
    (that floats up
through their miraculous
    bodies

and lingers above them
    in the gold air)
that won't live forever.

TWO PAINTINGS BY GUSTAV KLIMT

Although what glitters
on the trees
row after perfect row,
is merely
the injustice
of the world,

the chips on the bark of each
beech tree
catching the light, the sum
of these delays
is the beautiful, the human
beautiful,

body of flaws.
The dead
would give anything
I'm sure,
to step again onto
the leaf-rot,

into the avenue of mottled shadows,
the speckled
broken skins. The dead
in their sheer
open parenthesis, what they
wouldn't give

for something to lean on
    that won't
give way. I think I
    would weep
for the moral nature
    of this world,

for right and wrong like pools
    of shadow
and light you can step in
    and out of
crossing this yellow beech forest,
    this *buchen-wald*,

one autumn afternoon, late
    in the twentieth
century, in hollow light,
    in gaseous light. . . .
To receive the light
    and return it

and stand in rows, anonymous,
    is a sweet secret
even the air wishes
    it could unlock.
See how it pokes at them
    in little hooks,

the blue air, the yellow trees.
    Why be afraid?
They say when Klimt
    died suddenly
a painting, still
    incomplete,

was found in his studio,
    a woman's body
open at its point of
    entry,
rendered in graphic,
    pornographic,

detail—something like
    a scream
between her legs. Slowly,
    feathery,
he had begun to paint
    a delicate

garment (his trademark)
    over this mouth
of her body. The mouth
    of her face
is genteel, bored, feigning a need
    for sleep. The fabric

defines the surface,
    the story,
so we are drawn to it,
    its blues
and yellows glittering
    like a stand

of beech trees late
    one afternoon
in Germany, in fall.
    It is called

Buchenwald, it is
1890. In

the finished painting
the argument
has something to do
with pleasure.

AT LUCA SIGNORELLI'S RESURRECTION OF THE BODY

See how they hurry
    to enter
their bodies,
    these spirits.
Is it better, flesh,
    that they

should hurry so?
    From above
the green-winged angels
    blare down
trumpets and light. But
    they don't care,

they hurry to congregate,
    they hurry
into speech, until
    it's a marketplace,
it is humanity. But still
    we wonder

in the chancel
    of the dark cathedral,
is it better, back?
    The artist
has tried to make it so: each tendon
    they press

to re-enter

    is perfect. But is it

perfection

    they're after,

pulling themselves up

    through the soil

into the weightedness, the color,

    into the eye

of the painter? Outside

    it is 1500,

all round the cathedral

    streets hurry to open

through the wild

    silver grasses. . . .

The men and women

    on the cathedral wall

do not know how,

    having come this far,

to stop their

    hurrying. They amble off

in groups, in

    couples. Soon

some are clothed, there is

    distance, there is

perspective. Standing below them

    in the church

in Orvieto, how can we

    tell them

to be stern and brazen

    and slow,

that there is no
        entrance,
only entering. They keep on
        arriving,
wanting names,
        wanting

happiness. In his studio
        Luca Signorelli
in the name of God
        and Science
and the believable
        broke into the body

studying arrival.
        But the wall
of the flesh
        opens endlessly,
its vanishing point so deep
        and receding

we have yet to find it,
        to have it
stop us. So he cut
        deeper,
graduating slowly
        from the symbolic

to the beautiful. How far
        is true?
When his one son
        died violently,
he had the body brought to him
        and laid it

on the drawing-table,
 and stood
at a certain distance
 awaiting the best
possible light, the best depth
 of day,

then with beauty and care
 and technique
and judgment, cut into
 shadow, cut
into bone and sinew and every
 pocket

in which the cold light
 pooled.
It took him days
 that deep
caress, cutting,
 unfastening,

until his mind
 could climb into
the open flesh and
 mend itself.

from

THE END
OF BEAUTY

SELF-PORTRAIT AS THE GESTURE BETWEEN THEM

(Adam and Eve)

1

The gesture like a fruit torn from a limb, torn swiftly.

2

The whole bough bending then springing back as if from sudden sight.

3

The rip in the fabric where the action begins, the opening of the narrow passage.

4

The passage along the arc of dénouement once the plot has begun, like a limb,
the buds in it cinched and numbered,
outside the true story really, outside of improvisation,
moving along day by day into the sweet appointment.

5

But what else could they have done, these two, sick of beginning,
revolving in place like a thing seen,
dumb, blind, rooted in the eye that's watching,
ridden and ridden by that slowest of glances the passage of time
staring and staring until the entrails show.

6

Every now and then a quick rain for no reason,

7

a wind moving round all sides, a wind shaking the points of view out
like the last bits of rain. . . .

8

So it was to have freedom she did it but like a secret thought.
A thought of him the light couldn't touch.
The light beating against it, the light flaying her thought of him,
trying to break it.
Like a fruit that grows but only in the invisible.
The whole world of the given beating against this garden
where he walks slowly in the hands of freedom
noiselessly beating his steps against the soil.

9

But a secret grows, a secret wants to be given away.
For a long time it swells and stains its bearer with beauty.
It is what we see swelling forth making the shape we know a thing by.
The thing inside, the critique of the given.

10

So that she turned the thought of him in her narrow mind,
turned him slowly in the shallows, like a thin bird she'd found,
turned him in this place which was her own, as if to plant him but never
letting go,

keeping the thought of him keen and simple in a kind of winter,
keeping him in this shadowlessness in which he needn't breathe,
him turning to touch her as a thing turns towards its thief,
owned but not scizable, resembling, resembling. . . .

11

Meanwhile the heights of things were true. Meanwhile the distance of
the fields was true. Meanwhile the fretting of the light against the backs
of them
as they walked through the fields naming things, true,
the touch of the light along the backs of their bodies . . .

12

as the apple builds inside the limb, as rain builds
in the atmosphere, as the lateness accumulates until it finally
is,
as the meaning of the story builds,

13

scribbling at the edges of her body until it must be told, be

14

taken from her, this freedom,

15

so that she had to turn and touch him to give it away

16

to have him pick it from her as the answer takes the question

17

that he should read in her the rigid inscription

18

in a scintillant fold the fabric of the daylight bending

19

where the form is complete where the thing must be torn off

20

momentarily angelic, the instant writhing into a shape,

21

the two wedded, the readiness and the instant,

22

the extra bit that shifts the scales the other way now in his hand,
the gift that changes the balance,

23

the balance that cannot be broken owned by the air until he touches,

24

the balance like an apple held up into the sunlight

25

then taken down, the air changing by its passage, the feeling of being capable,

26

of being not quite right for the place, not quite the thing that's needed,

27

the feeling of being a digression not the link in the argument,
a new direction, an offshoot, the limb going on elsewhere,

28

and liking that error, a feeling of being capable *because* an error,

29

of being wrong perhaps altogether wrong a piece from another set

30

stripped of position stripped of true function

31

and loving that error, loving that filial form, that break from perfection

32

where the complex mechanism fails, where the stranger appears in the clearing,

33

out of nowhere and uncalled for, out of nowhere to share the day.

ORPHEUS AND EURYDICE

Up ahead, I know, he felt it stirring in himself already, the glance,
the darting thing in the pile of rocks,

already in him, there, shiny in the rubble, hissing Did you want to remain
completely unharmed?—

the point-of-view darting in him, shiny head in the ash-heap,

hissing Once upon a time, and then Turn now darling give me that look,

that perfect shot, give me that place where I'm erased. . . .

The thing, he must have wondered, could it be put to rest, there, in the
                                                                    glance,
could it lie back down into the dustiness, giving its outline up?

When we turn to them—limbs, fields, expanses of dust called meadow and
                                                                    avenue—
will they be freed then to slip back in?

Because you see he could not be married to it anymore, this field with
                                                                    minutes in it
called woman, its presence in him the thing called

future—could not be married to it anymore, expanse tugging his mind out
                                                                    into it,

tugging the wanting-to-finish out.

What he dreamed of was this road (as he walked on it), this dustiness,
but without their steps on it, their prints, without
song—

What she dreamed, as she watched him turning with the bend in the road
(can you
understand this?)—what she dreamed

was of disappearing into the seen

not of disappearing, lord, into the real—

And yes she could feel it in him already, up ahead, that wanting-to-turn-and-
cast-the-outline-over-her

by his glance,

sealing the edges down,

saying I know you from somewhere darling, don't I,
saying You're the kind of woman who etcetera—

(Now the cypress are swaying) (Now the lake in the distance)
(Now the view-from-above, the aerial attack of *do you
remember?*)—

now the glance reaching her shoreline wanting only to be recalled,
now the glance reaching her shoreline wanting only to be taken in,

(somewhere the castle above the river)

(somewhere you holding this piece of paper)

(what will you do next?) (—feel it beginning?)

now she's raising her eyes, as if pulled from above,

now she's looking back into it, into the poison the beginning,

giving herself to it, looking back into the eyes,

feeling the dry soft grass beneath her feet for the first time now the mind

looking into that which sets the _____ in motion and seeing in there

a doorway open nothing on either side
(a slight wind now around them, three notes from up the hill)

through which morning creeps and the first true notes—

For they were deep in the earth and what is possible swiftly took hold.

VERTIGO

Then they came to the very edge of the cliff and looked down.

Below a real world flowed in its parts, green, green.

The two elements touched—rock, air.

She thought of where the mind opened out

into the sheer drop of its intelligence,

the updrafting pastures of the vertical in which a bird now rose,

blue body the blue wind was knifing upward

faster than it could naturally rise,

up into the downdraft until it was frozen until she could see them

                                                    at last

the stages of flight, broken down, broken free,

each wingflap folding, each splay of the feather-sets flattening

for entry. . . . *Parts* she thought, *free parts*, watching the laws

at work, *through which desire must course*

seeking an ending, seeking a shape. Until the laws of flight and fall

                                                   increased.

Until they made, all of an instant, a bird, a blue

enchantment of properties no longer

knowable. What is it to understand, she let fly,

leaning outward from the edge now that the others had gone down.

How close can the two worlds get, the movement from one to the other

being death? She tried to remember from the other life

the passage of the rising notes off the violin

into the air, thin air, chopping their way in,

wanting to live forever—marrying, marrying—yet still free of the

                                              orchestral swelling

which would at any moment pick them up, incorporate. How is it one soul wants to be owned

by a single other

in its entirety?—

What is it sucks one down, offering itself, only itself, for

ever? She saw the cattle below

moving in a shape which was exactly their hunger.

She saw—could they be men?—the plot. She leaned. How does one enter

a story? Where the cliff and air pressed the end of each other,

everything else in the world—woods, fields, stream, start of another

                                        darker

woods—appeared as kinds of

falling. She listened for the wind again. What was it in there

                        she could hear

that has nothing to do with *telling the truth*?

What was it that was *not her listening*?

She leaned out. What is it pulls at one, she wondered,

what? That it has no shape but point of view?

That it cannot move to hold us?

Oh it has vibrancy, she thought, this emptiness, this intake just

                        prior to

the start of a story, the mind trying to fasten

and fasten, the mind feeling it like a sickness this wanting

to snag, catch hold, begin, the mind crawling out to the edge of the cliff

and feeling the body as if for the first time—how it cannot

follow, cannot love.

ON DIFFICULTY

It's that they want to know *whose* they are,

seen from above in the half burnt-out half blossomed-out

woods, late April, unsure as to whether to

turn back.

The woods are not their home.

The blossoming is not their home. Whatever's back there

is not. Something floats in the air all round them

as if *it* were the place

where the day drowns,

and the place at the edge of cries, for instance, that fissure, gleams.

Now he's holding his hand out.

Is there a hollow she's the shape of?

And in their temples a thrumming like

what-have-I-done?—but not yet a question, really, not

yet what slips free of the voice to float like a brackish foam

on emptiness—

Oh you will come to it, you two down there

where the vines begin, you will come to it,

the thing towards which you reason, the place where the flotsam

of the meanings is put down

and the shore

holds. They're thinking *we must have slept a while,*

what is it has changed? They're thinking

how low the bushes are, after all, how finite

the options one finds in the

waiting (after all). More like the branchings of whiteness

always stopping short into this shade or that,

breaking inertia then stopping,

breaking the current at last into shape but then

stopping—

If you asked them, where they first find the edges of each other's bodies, *where*

happiness resides they'd look up through the gap

in the greenery you're looking down through.

What they want to know—the icons silent in the shut church (to the left),

the distance silent in the view (to the right)—

is how to give themselves *away*,

which is why they look up now,

which is why they'll touch each other now (for your

looking), which is why they want to know what this

reminds you of

looking up, reaching each other for you to see, for you to see by, the long sleep

beginning, the long sleep of resemblance,

touching each other further for you that eternity begin, there, between you,

letting the short jabs of grass hold them up for you to count by,

to color the scene into the believable by,

letting the thousands of individual blossoms add up

and almost (touching her further) block your view of them—

When you look away

who will they be dear god and what?

WHAT THE END IS FOR

(Grand Forks, North Dakota)

A boy just like you took me out to see them,
    the five hundred B-52's on alert on the runway,
fully loaded fully manned pointed in all the directions,
    running every minute
of every day.
    They sound like a sickness of the inner ear,

where the heard foams up into the noise of listening,
    where the listening arrives without being extinguished.
The huge hum soaks up into the dusk.
    The minutes spring open. Six is too many.
From where we watch,
    from where even watching is an anachronism,

from the 23rd of March from an open meadow,
    the concertina wire in its double helix
designed to tighten round a body if it turns
    is the last path the sun can find to take out,
each barb flaring gold like a braille being read,
    then off with its knowledge and the sun
is gone. . . .

That's when the lights on all the extremities, like an outline like a dress,
    become loud in the story,
and a dark I have not seen before

sinks in to hold them one

by one.

    Strange plot made to hold so many inexhaustible

screams.

    Have you ever heard in a crowd mutterings of

blame

that will not modulate that will not rise?

    He tells me, your stand-in, they *stair-step* up.

He touches me to have me look more deeply

    in

to where for just a moment longer

    color still lives:

the belly white so that it looks like sky, the top

    some kind of brown, some soil—How does it look

from up there now

    this meadow we lie on our bellies in, this field Iconography

tells me stands for sadness

    because the wind can move through it uninterrupted?

What is it the wind

    would have wanted to find and didn't

leafing down through this endless admiration unbroken

    because we're too low for it

to find us?

    Are you still there for me now in that dark

we stood in for hours

    letting it sweep as far as it could down over us

unwilling to move, irreconcilable? What *he*

    wants to tell me,

his whisper more like a scream

    over this eternity of engines never not running,

is everything: how the crews assigned to each plane

    for a week at a time, the seven boys, must live

inseparable,

    how they stay together for life,

how the wings are given a life of

    seven feet of play,

how they drop practice bombs called *shapes* over Nevada,

    how the measures for counterattack in air

have changed and we

    now forgo firepower for jamming, for the throwing

of false signals. The meadow, the meadow hums, love, with the planes,

    as if every last blade of grass were wholly possessed

by this practice, wholly prepared. The last time I saw you,

    we stood facing each other as dusk came on.

I leaned against the refrigerator, you leaned against the door.

    The picture window behind you was slowly extinguished,

the tree went out, the two birdfeeders, the metal braces on them.

    The light itself took a long time,

bits in puddles stuck like the useless

    splinters of memory, the chips

of history, hopes, laws handed down. *Here, hold these* he says, these

    grasses these

torn pods, he says, smiling over the noise another noise, *take these*

    he says, my hands wrong for

the purpose, here,

    not-visible-from-the-sky, prepare yourself with these, boy and

bouquet of

thistleweed and wort and william and

timothy. We stood there. Your face went out a long time

    before the rest of it. Can't see you anymore I said. *Nor I,*

you, whatever you still were

    replied.

When I asked you to hold me you refused.

    When I asked you to cross the six feet of room to hold me

you refused. Until I

    couldn't rise out of the patience either any longer

to make us

    take possession.

Until we were what we must have wanted to be:

    shapes the shapelessness was taking back.

Why should I lean out?

    Why should I move?

When the Maenads tear Orpheus limb from limb,

    they throw his head

out into the river.

    Unbodied it sings

all the way downstream, all the way to the single ocean,

    head floating in current downriver singing,

until the sound of the cataracts grows,

    until the sound of the open ocean grows and the voice.

SELF-PORTRAIT AS APOLLO AND DAPHNE

1

The truth is this had been going on for a long time during which
    they both wanted it to last.

You can still hear them in that phase, the north and
south laid up against each other, constantly erasing
each minute with each minute.

You can still hear them, there, just prior to daybreak,
the shrill cheeps and screeches of the awakening thousands,
hysterical, for miles, in all the directions,

and there the *whoo whoo* of the nightfeeders, insolvent baseline,
shorn, almost the sound of thin air. . . .

Or there where the sun picks up on the bits of broken glass
throughout the miles of grass for just a fraction of an instant
(thousands of bits) at just one angle, quick, the evidence,
    the landfill,
then gone again, everything green, green. . . .

2

How he wanted, though, to possess her, to nail the erasures,

3

like a long heat on her all day once the daysounds set in, like
a long analysis.

4

The way she kept slipping away was this: can you really
see me, can you really know I'm really who . . .
His touchings a rhyme she kept interrupting (no one
believes in that version anymore she whispered, no one
can hear it anymore, *tomorrow, tomorrow,*
like the different names of those girls
all one girl). . . . But how long could it
last?

5

He kept after her like sunlight (it's not what you think, she said)
frame after frame of it (it's not what you think you think)
like the prayer that numbers are praying (are they ascending are they
descending?)

He kept after her in the guise of the present,
minute after minute (are they ascending are they?)
until they seemed to quicken and narrow (like footprints

piling up, like footprints all blurred at the end of, at the scene of . . .)

until *now is forever* he whispered can't you get it to open,

present tense without end, slaughtered motion, kingdom of
heaven?—

6

the shards caught here and there—*what did you do*
before? or *will you forgive me?* or *say*
that you'll love me for

ever and ever

(is it a squeal of brakes is it a birthcry?)

(let x equal forever he whispered let y let y . . .)

7

as opposed to that other motion which reads Cast it upon the ground
and it shall become a serpent (and Moses fled before it),
which reads Put forth thy hand and take it by the tail
and it was a rod in his hand again—

8

That's when she stopped, she turned her face to the wind, shut her eyes—

9

She stopped she turned,
she would not be the end towards which he was ceaselessly tending,
she would not give shape to his hurry by being
    its destination,
it was wrong this progress, it was a quick iridescence
on the back of some other thing, unimaginable, a flash on the wing of . . .

10

The sun would rise and the mind would rise
and the will would rise and the eyes—The eyes—:
the whole of the story like a transcript of sight,
of the distance between them, the small gap he would close.

11

She would stop, there would be no chase scene, she would
    be who,
what?

12

The counting went on all round like a thousand birds
each making its own wind—who would ever add them up?—

and what would the sum become, of these minutes, each flapping
its wings, each after a perch,

each one with its call going unanswered,

each one signaling separately into the end of the daybreak,

the great screech of the instants, the pile-up,
the one math of hope, the prayer nowhere is praying,

frame after frame, collision of tomorrows—

No she would go under, she would leave him in the freedom

his autograph all over it, slipping, trying to notch it,

13

there in the day with him now, his day, but altered,

14

part of the view not one of the actors, she thought,

not one of the instances, not one of the examples,

15

but the air the birds call in,
the air their calls going unanswered marry in,
the calls the different species make, cross-currents, frettings,
and the one air holding the screeching separateness—
each wanting to change, to be heard, to have been changed—
and the air all round them neither full nor empty,
but holding them, holding them, untouched, untransformed.

NOLI ME TANGERE

1

You see the angels have come to sit on the delay
    for a while,
they have come to harrow the fixities, the sharp edges
    of this open
sepulcher,
    they have brought their swiftnesses like musics

down
    to fit them on the listening.
Their robes, their white openmindedness gliding into the corners,
    slipping this way then that
over the degrees, over the marble

flutings.
    The small angelic scripts pressing up through the veils.
The made shape pressing
    up through the windy cloth.
I've watched all afternoon how the large
    red birds here

cross and recross neither for play nor hunger
    the gaps that constitute our chainlink fence,
pressing themselves narrowly against the metal,
    feeding their bodies and wings

tightly in.

    Out of what ceases into what is ceasing.

Out of the light which holds steel and its alloys,

into the words for it like some robe or glory,

    and all of this rising up into the deep unbearable thinness,

the great babyblue exhalation of the one God

    as if in satisfaction at some right ending

come,

then down onto the dustiness that still somehow holds

    its form as downslope and new green meadow

through which at any moment

    something swifter

might cut.

    It is about to be

Spring.

    The secret cannot be

kept.

    It wants to cross over, it wants

to be a lie.

2

Is that it then? Is that the law of freedom?

    That she must see him yet must not touch?

Below them the soldiers sleep their pure deep sleep.

    Is he light

who has turned forbidding and thrust his hand up

    in fury,

is he flesh

    so desperate to escape, to carry his purpose away?

She wants to put her hands in,

    she wants to touch him.

He wants her to believe,

    who has just trusted what her eyes have given her,

he wants her to look away.

    I've listened where the words and the minutes would touch,

I've tried to hear in that slippage what

    beauty is—

her soil, his sweet tune like footsteps

    over the path of

least resistance. I can see

    the body composed

of the distance between them.

    I know it is ours: he must change, she must

remember.

    But you see it is not clear to me why she

must be driven back,

    why it is the whole darkness that belongs to her

and its days,

    why it is these hillsides she must become,

supporting even now the whole weight of the weightless,

    letting the plotlines wander all over her,

crumbling into every digressive beauty,

    her longings all stitchwork towards his immaculate rent,

all alphabet on the wind as she rises from prayer. . . .

It is the horror, Destination,
    pulling the whole long song
down, like a bad toss
    let go
in order to start again right,
    and it is wrong

to let its one inaudible note govern our going
    isn't it, siren over this open meadow
singing always your one song of shape of
    home. I have seen how the smoke here
inhabits a space
    in the body of air it must therefore displace,

and the tree-shaped gap the tree inhabits,
    and the tree-shaped gap the tree
invents. Siren,
    reader,
it is here, only here,
    in this gap

between us,
    that the body of who we are
to have been
    emerges: imagine:
she lets him go,
    she lets him through the day faster than the day,

among the brisk wings
    upsetting the flowerpots,
among the birds arranging and rearranging the shape of

the delay,
she lets him
slip free,

letting him posit the sweet appointment,
letting out that gold thread that crazy melody
of stations,
reds, birds, dayfall, screen-door,
desire,

until you have to go with him, don't you,

until you have to leave her be
if all you have to touch her with
is form.

SELF-PORTRAIT AS HURRY AND DELAY

(Penelope at Her Loom)

1

So that every night above them in her chambers she unweaves it.
Every night by torchlight under the flitting shadows the postponement,
working her fingers into the secret place, the place of what is coming
    undone,

2

to make them want her more richly, there, where the pattern softens now,
    loosening,

3

to see what was healed under there by the story when it lifts,
by color and progress and motive when they lift,

4

the bandage the history gone into thin air,

5

to have them for an instant in her hands both at once,
the story and its undoing, the days the kings and the soil they're groundcover
    for

6

all winter,

7

against choice against offspring against the minutes like turrets
building the walls, the here and the there, in which he wanders searching,

8

till it lifts and the mouth of something fangs open there,
and the done and the undone rush into each other's arms.
A *mouth* or a gap in the fleshy air, a place in both worlds.
A woman's body, a spot where a story now gone has ridden.
The yarn springing free.
The opening trembling, the nothing, the nothing with use in it trembling—

9

Oh but is it wide enough to live on, immaculate present tense, lull
      between wars,

10

the threads running forwards yet backwards over her stilled fingers,

11

the limbs of the evergreens against the windowpane, the thousand hands, beating then touching then suddenly still for no reason?

12

Reader, minutes:

13

now her fingers dart as his hurry darts over this openness he can't
    find the edge of,
like the light over the water seeking the place on the water
where out of air and point-of-view and roiling wavetips a shapeliness,
    a possession of happiness
forms,

a body of choices among the waves, a strictness among them, an edge
    to the light,

something that is not something else,

14

until she knows he's here who wants to be trapped in here,
her hands tacking his quickness down as if soothing it to sleep,
the threads carrying the quickness in on their backs,
burying it back into there, into the pattern, the noble design,
like a stain they carry past a sleeping giant,
the possible like kindling riding in on their backs,
the flames enlarging and gathering on the walls,
wanting to be narrowed, rescued, into a story again, a transparence we
can't see through, a lover

15

approaching ever approaching the unmade beneath him,
knotting and clasping it within his motions,
wrapping himself plot plot and dénouement over the roiling openness. . . .

16

Yet what would she have if he were to arrive?
Sitting enthroned what would either have?
It is his wanting in the threads she has to keep alive for him,
scissoring and spinning and pulling the long minutes free, it is

17

the shapely and mournful delay she keeps alive for him the breathing

18

as the long body of the beach grows emptier awaiting him

19

gathering the holocaust in close to its heart growing more beautiful

20

under the meaning under the soft hands of its undoing

21

saying Goodnight goodnight for now going upstairs

22

under the kissing of the minutes under the wanting to go on living

23

beginning always beginning the ending as they go to sleep beneath her.

BREAKDANCING

(Teresa: Saint Teresa of Ávila)

Staying alive the boy on the screen is doing it,
    the secret nobody knows like a rapture through his limbs,
the secret, *the robot-like succession of joint isolations*
    that simulate a body's reaction to
electric shock.
    This is how it tells itself: pops, ticks, waves and the

float. What
    is poverty for, Mr. Speed, Dr. Cadet, Dr. Rage,
Timex? Don't push me the limbs are whispering, don't push
    'cause I'm close to the edge the footwork is whispering
down onto the sidewalk that won't give in won't go some other
    where while the TV

hums and behind me their breathings, husband, daughter, too slow,
    go in to that other place and come back out
unstained, handfuls at a time, air, air—
    The flag of the greatest democracy on earth
waves in the wind with the sound turned off. The current

rubs through the stars and stripes
    like a muttering passing through a crowd and coming out an
anthem,
    string of words on its search
and destroy

needing bodies, bodies. . . .
I'm listening to where she must not choke. I'm listening
    to where he must not be betrayed. I'm trying

to hear pity, the idiom. I'm trying to lean into those
    marshes and hear
what comes through clean,
    what comes through changed,
having needed us.
    Oh but you must not fail to eat and sleep Teresa murmurs to
her flock,

staying alive is the most costly gift you have to offer Him—all the while
                                          watching,
    (whispering Lord, what will you have me
do?) for his corporal
    appearance
in the light of the sixteenth century, in the story that flutters
    blowzy over the body of the land
we must now somehow ram
    the radioactive waste

into. He
    showed himself to her in pieces.
First the fingertips, there in mid-air,
    clotting, floating, held up by the invisible, neither rising
nor falling nor approaching nor lingering, then hands, then a

few days later feet, torso, then arms, each part alone, each part
    free of its argument, then days, then eyes,
then face entire, then days again, then *His*
    most sacred humanity in its risen form
was represented to me

completely. "Don't try

    to hold me in yourself (the air, hissing) but try to hold yourself

in me," Nov 18, 1570. I'm listening to where she must not choke,

    I'm listening to where he must not, must not. . . . Air,

holding a girl in a man's arms now,

    making them look like wind,

what if they can't be returned to you

    the *things* now reaching me—the three

exhalings, hum, blue light, the minutes, the massacres, the strict half-life of

    radioactive isotopes, the shallow

graves, the seventeen rememberable personal

    lies? What if they go only this far, grounding

in me, staying

    alive?

Here is the secret: the end is an animal.

    Here is the secret: the end is an animal growing by

accretion, image by image, vote by

    vote. *No more pain* hums the air,

as the form of things shall have fallen

    from thee, no more pain, just the here and the now, the jackpot, the

watching, minutes exploding like thousands of silver dollars all over your

    face your hands but tenderly, almost tenderly, turning mid-air, gleaming,

so slow, as if it could last,

    frame after frame of nowhere

turning into the living past.

SELF-PORTRAIT AS DEMETER AND PERSEPHONE

1

So Look I said this is the burning bush we're in it it has three faces

It's a day's work it's the hand that takes and the other one

The other one the mother the one whose grief is the visible world

a wound she must keep open by beginning and beginning

2

Oh but you have to learn to let her go you said
out into the open field through the waiting the waving grasses
way out to the edge of that drastic field of distinctions
each new possibility molting off the back of the one motion, creation,
until there are so many truths each one its own color
it's a flower the picking of which would open the world
the mouth over the unsaid whispering loves me not loves me

Out alone in the field us watching her from a distance

Can she still find the way are the cracks small enough?

3

Meanwhile up here now this is the knowable
clucking I've been looking for you all day clucking I

will not remember O Lord for it will be taken from me
And the meekness shall be the absence of testimony
the eyes that look neither towards nor away
four jays on the hedgerows four blue-gray-black mutterings
and the miles stretched out to tempt the mind into them
tugging and tugging is it beautiful can she hear us?

4

Underneath she was gone into the fire the absence of the past
to where you pay what you owe then you want to pay more
She took off the waiting she stood before him without nouns
He held her where are the images he said we will destroy them
you are in hell now there is no beginning

the outline is a creature that will blur you will forget him

as for motive that shapeliness let us splinter it let us scatter it

there is no reason for this that's what your body is for

5

She watched the smoke where it began what it left off
What will I recognize it to have been she thought
smoke smoke her fingers her eyes like static all over it
Surely I can find it the point of departure she put her hand in
The birds the beaks of the birds the song the heard song
She reached in what is it begins at the end she thought
Where is the skin of the minutes will it ever come off
She reached in there was no underneath what was this coiling
    over her fingers
She reached in she could go no further she was sealed off

It pushed back against her it was hell she could finally lean
It was the given and it was finally given

or is it, or is it. . . . It was then she remembered

slit   hum   mob   wing of

and you what did you do? For a long time I

6

It was then she remembered and looked the other way

7

Why this sky why this air why these mountains why this sky

8

And what does he ask of you, only to fear Him

9

Where does the air end? Where does the sky begin?
She saw the made grieving above her like a mother or winter
the great gap grieving all form and shadow
heard the god of the place lean down and describe the grief:
and he shall be to thee in stead of a mouth and thou shalt be to him
in stead of God

(why should she come back up why should she begin again)

10

Look she said I have to go back now if you don't mind waiting
But tell me, those minutes whispering Behold the day shall come
are they confounded or do they begin again from scratch each instant
from scratch from dirt like a confession under unbearable torture?

He said Look this is the burning bush we're in it it has two faces

11

Neither toward nor away the crack opened she surfaced
Where she surfaced it's all the same it's always been so why try
she felt her mother in her body it was easy not to worry
the light flayed her she was a new woman she could inhabit a shape
Minutes go in Words come out A machine for waiting

12

The first thing she saw when she surfaced was the wind
wrapping like a body round the stiff stripped trees
that would bend more deeply into that love if they could
to accompany its eagerness young wind its rage
if they weren't so perfect if they weren't so shorn

13

(the tinfoil winking in the snowmelt the rinds)

14

that would bend more deeply into it inventing (if they could)

15

another body, exploded, all leafiness, unimaginable

16

by which to be forgiven by which to suffer completely this wind

OF FORCED SIGHTES AND TRUSTY FEREFULNESS

Stopless wind, here are the columbine seeds I have
collected. What we would do with them is
different. Though both your trick and mine flowers blue
and white

with four stem tails and yellow underpetals. Stopless
and unessential, half-hiss, half-
lullaby, if I fell in among your laws,
if I fell down into your mind your snow, into the miles

of spirit-drafts you drive, frenetic multitudes,
out from timber to the open ground and back to no
avail, if I fell down, warmblooded, ill, into your endless
evenness,

into this race you start them on and will not let them win . . . ?
If I fell in?
What is your law to my law, unhurried hurrying?
At my remove from you, today, in your supremest

calculation, re-
adjustment, are these three birds scratching for dead
bark beetles, frozen seeds, too late for being here yet only
        here,
in the stenchfree

cold. This is another current, river of rivers, this thrilling
third-act love. Who wouldn't want to stay
behind? They pack the rinds away, the blazing applecores,
the frantic shadow-wings scribbling the fenceposts, window-

panes. Meanwhile you turn, white jury, draft, away,
deep justice done.
I don't presume to cross the distances, the clarity,
but what grows in your only open hands? Or is

digressive love,
row after perfect greenhouse row,
the garden you're out of for good, wind of the theorems,
of proof, square root of light,

chaos of truth,
blinder than the mice that wait you out
    in any crack?
This is the best I can do now for prayer—to you,
for you—these scraps I throw

my lonely acrobats
that fall
of your accord
right to my windowsill: they pack it away, the grains, the

accidents, they pack it deep into the rent
heart of the blue
spruce, skins in with spiky needles. . . . Oh
    hollow
charged with forgetfulness,

through wind, through winter nights, we'll pass,
steering with crumbs, with words,
making of every hour
a thought, remembering

by pain and rhyme and arabesques of foraging
the formula for theft
under your sky that keeps
sliding away

married to hurry
and grim song.

from

REGION OF
UNLIKENESS

FISSION

   The real electric lights light upon the full-sized
screen
      on which the greater-than-life-size girl appears,
almost nude on the lawn—sprinklers on—
      voice-over her mother calling her name out—loud—
camera angle giving her lowered lids their full
      expanse—a desert—as they rise

out of the shabby annihilation,
      out of the possibility of never-having-been-seen,
and rise,
      till the glance is let loose into the auditorium,
and the man who has just stopped in his tracks
      looks down
for the first

      time. Tick tock. It's the birth of the mercantile
dream (he looks down). It's the birth of
      the dream called
new world (looks down). She lies there. A corridor of light
                                    filled with dust
      flows down from the booth to the screen.
Everyone in here wants to be taken off

      somebody's list, wants to be placed on
somebody else's list.
      Tick. It is 1963. The idea of history is being
outmaneuvered.
      So that as the houselights come on—midscene—

not quite killing the picture which keeps flowing beneath,

     a man comes running down the aisle
asking for our attention—
     Ladies and Gentlemen.
I watch the houselights lap against the other light—the tunnel
     of image-making dots licking the white sheet awake—
a man, a girl, her desperate mother—daisies growing in the
                       corner—

     I watch the light from our real place
suck the arm of screen-building light into itself
     until the gesture of the magic forearm frays,
and the story up there grays, pales—them almost lepers now,
                 saints, such
white on their flesh in
     patches—her thighs like receipts slapped down on a
              slim silver tray,

her eyes as she lowers the heart-shaped shades,
     as the glance glides over what used to be the open,
the free,
     as the glance moves, pianissimo, over the glint of day,
over the sprinkler, the mother's voice shrieking like a grappling
     hook,
the grass blades aflame with being-seen, here on the out-

     skirts. . . . You can almost hear the click at the heart of
              the silence
where the turnstile shuts and he's *in*—our hero—
     the moment spoked,
our gaze on her fifteen-foot eyes,

the man hoarse now as he waves his arms,

as he screams to the booth to cut it, cut the sound,

and the sound is cut,

and her sun-barred shoulders are left to turn

soundless as they accompany

her neck, her face, the

looking-up.

Now the theater's skylight is opened and noon slides in.

I watch as it overpowers the electric lights,

whiting the story out one layer further

till it's just a smoldering of whites

where she sits up, and her stretch of flesh

is just a roiling up of graynesses,

vague stutterings of

light with motion in them, bits of moving zeros

in the infinite virtuality of light,

some *likeness* in it but not particulate,

a grave of possible shapes called *likeness*—see it?—something

scrawling up there that could be skin or daylight or even

the expressway now that he's gotten her to leave with him—

(it happened rather fast) (do you recall)—

the man up front screaming the President's been shot, waving

his hat, slamming one hand flat

over the open

to somehow get

our attention,

in Dallas, behind him the scorcher—whites, grays,

laying themselves across his face—

him like a beggar in front of us, holding his hat—
    I don't recall what I did,
I don't recall what the right thing to do would be,
    I wanted someone to love. . . .

    There is a way she lay down on that lawn
to begin with,
    in the heart of the sprinklers,
before the mother's call,
    before the man's shadow laid itself down,

there is a way to not yet be wanted,

    there is a way to lie there at twenty-four frames
per second—no faster—
    not at the speed of plot,
not at the speed of desire—

    the road out—expressway—hotels—motels—
no telling what we'll have to see next,
    no telling what all we'll have to want next
(right past the stunned rows of houses),
    no telling what on earth we'll have to marry marry marry. . . .

Where the three lights merged:
    where the image licked my small body from the front, the story
                        playing
all over my face my
    forwardness,
where the electric lights took up the back and sides,
    the unwavering houselights,
seasonless,

where the long thin arm of day came in from the top
to touch my head,
reaching down along my staring face—
where they flared up around my body unable to

merge into each other
over my likeness,
slamming down one side of me, unquenchable—here static

there flaming—
sifting grays into other grays—
mixing the split second into the long haul—
flanking me—undressing something there where my
body is
though not my body—
where they play on the field of my willingness,

where they kiss and brood, filtering each other to no avail,
all over my solo
appearance,
bits smoldering under the shadows I make—
and aimlessly—what we call *free*—there

the immobilism sets in,
the being-in-place more alive than the being,
my father sobbing beside me, the man on the stage
screaming, the woman behind us starting to
pray,
the immobilism, the being-in-place more alive than

the being,
the squad car now faintly visible on the screen
starting the chase up,

all over my countenance,
the velvet armrest at my fingers, the dollar bill

in my hand,
    choice the thing that wrecks the sensuous here the glorious here—
that wrecks the beauty,
    choice the move that rips the wrappings of light, the ever-tighter
                        wrappings of

the layers of
    the real: what is, what also is, what might be that is,
what could have been that is, what
    might have been that is, what I say that is,
what the words say that is,
    what you imagine the words say that is—Don't move, don't

wreck the shroud, don't move—

AT THE CABARET *NOW*

The Americans are lonely. They don't know what happened.
They're still up and there's all this time yet to kill.
The musicians are still being paid so they keep on.
The sax pants up the ladder, up.
They want to be happy. They want to just let the notes
come on, the mortal wounds, it's all been
paid for so what the hell, each breath going up, up,
them thinking of course Will he make it How far can he
go? Skill, the prince of the kingdom, there at *his* table
now.
Is there some other master, also there, at a
back table, a regular, one we can't make out
but whom the headwaiter knows, the one who never
applauds?
So that it's not about the ending, you see, or where to go
from here.
It's about the breath and how it reaches the trumpeter's hands,
how the hands come so close to touching the breath,
and how the gold thing, gleaming, is there in between,
the only avenue—the long way—captivity.
Like this thing now, slow, extending the metaphor to make a
place. Pledge allegiance. By which is meant
see, here, what a variety tonight, what a good crowd,
some of them saying yes, yes, some others no,
don't they sound good together?
And all around this, space, and seedspores,

and the green continuance.

And all along the musicians still getting paid so let them.

And all around that the motionlessness—

don't think about it though, because you can't.

And then the mother who stayed at home of course because her body . . .

Farewell.

Farewell.

This is the story of a small strict obedience.

Human blood.

And how it rivered into all its bloods.

Small stream, really, in the midst of the other ones.

In it children laughing and laughing which is the sound of

ripening.

Which the musicians can't play—but that is another

tale.

Someone invited them in, humanity, and they came in.

They said they knew and then they knew.

They made this bank called justice and then this other one

called not.

They swam in the river although sometimes it was notes.

And some notes are true, even now, yes.

They knew each other, then winter came

which was a curtain, and then spring which was when they realized

it was a curtain.

Which leads us to this, the showstopper: summer, the Americans.

I wish I could tell you the story—so and so holding his glass up,

the table around him jittery,

and how then *she* came along gliding between the tables

whispering *it exists*—enough to drive them all mad of course—

whispering *sharp as salt*, whispering *straw on fire looking at you*—

the Americans whispering it cannot be, stay where you are—

and the one in the back no one knows starting up the applause,

alone,

a flat sound like flesh beating flesh but only *like* it.

Tell me,

why did we live, lord?

Blood in a wind,

why were we meant to live?

FROM THE NEW WORLD

Has to do with the story about the girl who didn't die
    in the gas chamber, who came back out asking
for her mother. Then the moment—the next coil—where the guard,
    Ivan, since the 50's an autoworker in Cleveland,
orders a man on his way in to rape her.
    Then the narrowing, the tightening, but not in hunger, no,—the
                           witness

recollecting this on the stand somewhere in Israel in
    February 87 should You be keeping
track. Has to do with her coming back out? Asking for her mother?
    Can you help me in this?
Are you there in your stillness? Is it a real place?
    God knows I too want the poem to continue,

want the silky swerve into shapeliness
    and then the click shut
and then the issue of sincerity, the glossy diamond-backed
    skin—will you buy me, will you take me home. . . . About the one
who didn't die, her face still there on the new stalk of her body as the
    doors open,

the one who didn't like a relentless treble coming back out
    right here into the thing we call
daylight but which is what now, unmoored?
    The one time I knew something about us
though I couldn't say what

my grandmother then already ill

    took me by the hand asking to be introduced.

And then *no, you are not Jorie—but thank you for*

    saying you are. No. I'm sure. I know her you

see. I went into the bathroom, locked the door.

    Stood in front of the mirrored wall—

not so much to see in, not looking up at all in fact,

    but to be held in it as by a gas,

the thing which was me there in its chamber. Reader,

    they were all in there, I didn't look up,

they were all in there, the coiling and uncoiling

    billions,

the about-to-be-seized,

    the about to be held down,

the about to be held down, bit clean, shaped,

    and the others, too, the ones gone back out, the ending

wrapped round them,

    hands up to their faces why I don't know,

and the about-to-be stepping in,

    one form at a time stepping in as if to stay clean,

stepping over something to get into here,

    something there on the floor now dissolving,

not looking down but stepping up to clear it,

and clearing it,

    stepping in.

Without existence and then with existence.

    Then into the clearing as it clamps down

all round,

then into the fable as it clamps down.

    We put her in a Home, mother paid.

We put him in a Home, mother paid.

    There wasn't one that would take both of them we
could afford.

    We were right we put him down the road it's all
there was,

    there was a marriage of fifty years, you know this

already don't you fill in the blanks,

    they never saw each other again,

paralyzed on his back the last few years

    he bribed himself a private line, he rigged the phone so he

could talk, etcetera, you know this,

    we put her in X, she'd fallen out we put her back in,

there in her diaper sitting with her purse in her hands all day every

    day, asking can I go now,

meaning him, meaning the

    apartment by then long since let go you know this

don't you, shifting wind sorting and re-sorting the stuff, flesh,

    now the sunstruck field beyond her window,

now her hands on the forties sunburst silver

    clasp, the white patent-leather pocketbook—

I stood there. Let the silver down all over my shoulders.

    The sink. The goldspeck formica. The water
uncoiling.

    Then the click like a lock being tried.

Then the hollow caressing the back of my neck.

    Then the whole thing like a benediction you can't
shake off,

    and the eyes unfastening, nervous, as if they smelled something up there and had to go (don't wait for me), the

eyes lifting, up into the decoration, the eyes

    looking. Poor thing.

As if real. As if *in* the place.

    The twitch where the eyes meet the eyes.

A blush.

    You see it's not the matter of her coming back out

alive, is it?

    It's the asking-for. The please.

Isn't it?

    Then the man standing up, the witness, screaming it's him it's him

I'm sure your Honor I'm sure. Then Ivan coming up to him

    and Ivan (you saw this) offering his hand, click, whoever

he is, and the old man getting a dial-tone, friend,

    and old whoever clicking and unclicking the clasp the

silver knobs,

    shall we end on them? a tracking shot? a

close-up on the clasp a two-headed beast it turns out

    made of silvery

leaves? Where would you go now? *Where*

    screaming it's him it's

him? At the point where she comes back out something begins, yes,

    something new, something completely

new, but what—there underneath the screaming—what?

Like what, I wonder, to make the bodies come on, to make

    room,

like what, I whisper,

like which is the last new world, *like*, *like*, which is the thin

young body (before it's made to go back in) whispering *please.*

THE HIDING PLACE

The last time I saw it was 1968.
Paris France. The time of the *disturbances*.
    We had claims. Schools shut down.
A million *workers* and *students* on strike.

    Marches, sit-ins, helicopters, gas.
They stopped you at gunpoint asking for papers.

    I spent 11 nights sleeping in the halls. Arguments. *Negotiations.*
Hurrying in the dawn looking for a certain leader
    I found his face above an open streetfire.
No he said, tell them *no concessions.*
    His voice above the fire as if there were no fire—

language floating everywhere above the sleeping bodies;
    and crates of fruit donated in secret;
and torn sheets (for tear gas) tossed down from shuttered windows;
    and bread; and blankets; stolen from the firehouse.

The CRS (the government police) would swarm in around dawn
    in small blue vans and round us up.
Once I watched the searchbeams play on some flames.
    The flames push up into the corridor of light.

In the cell we were so crowded no one could sit or lean.
    People peed on each other. I felt a girl
vomiting gently onto my back.
    I found two Americans rounded up by chance,

their charter left that morning they screamed, what were they going to

do?

Later a man in a uniform came in with a stick.

Started beating here and there, found the girl in her eighth month.

He beat her frantically over and over.

He pummeled her belly. Screaming aren't you ashamed?

I remember the cell vividly

but is it from a photograph? I think the shadows as I

see them still—the slatted brilliant bits

against the wall—I think they're true—but are they from a photograph?

Do I see it from inside now—his hands, her face—or

is it from the news account?

The strangest part of getting out again was *streets*.

The light running down them.

Everything spilling whenever the wall breaks.

And the air—thick with dwellings—the air filled—doubled—

as if the open

had been made to render—

The open squeezed for space until the hollows spill out,

story upon story of them.

starting to light up as I walked out.

How thick was the empty meant to be?

What were we finding in the air?

What were we meant to find?

I went home slowly sat in my rented room.

Sat for a long time the window open,

watched the white gauze curtain sluff this way then that

a bit—

watched the air suck it out, push it back in. Lung

of the room with streetcries in it. Watched until the lights

    outside made it gold, pumping gently.

Was I meant to get up again? I was inside. The century clicked by.

    The woman below called down *not to forget the*

    loaf. Crackle of helicopters. Voice on a loudspeaker issuing

warnings.

    They made agreements we all returned to work.

The government fell but then it was all right again.

    The man above the fire, listening to my question,

the red wool shirt he wore: where is it? who has it?

    He looked straight back into the century: no concessions.

I took the message back.

    The look in his eyes—shoving out—into the open—

                expressionless with thought:

no—tell them *no*—

PICNIC

The light shone down taking the shape of each lie,
    lifting each outline up, making it wear a name.
It was one day near the very end of childhood, Rome,
    out on a field late April, parents, friends,
after a morning's walk (nearing mid-century),
    some with baskets, some with hats,

(so does it matter that this be true?) some
    picking flowers, meaning by that a door that does not open—
And why should I tell this to you,
    and why should *telling* matter still, the bringing to life of
listening, the party going on down there, grasses,
    voices? Should I tell you who they are, there on the torn

page—should we count them (nine)—and then the girl who
                                     was me
    at the edge of the blanket,
two walking off towards what sounds like a stream now?
    Pay attention. Years pass. They are still there.
And the sorrow kept under. And the quick jagged laughs.
    And all the while underneath something else is meant—

the *ladder with no rungs* perhaps, or *things*
    exist?
Meanwhile the wind bends the grasses flat then up again, like that,
    and at the picnic someone's laugh breaks off the mouth
and comes to this.
    Waiting is different from patience, friend. This

is the picnic.

    "Unminding mind, keep in the middle—until" says the silly
                                           book where

"Shiva Replies".

    In the field four bluebirds land. *Flish.*

Then no wind for a moment.

    Then someone's laugh, although they are lying,

and X who will sleep with father

later this afternoon.

    The mouths of the gods are stuck open really.

They are sated, exhausted, and still they must devour us.

    After lunch we take a walk.

We walk into their eyes, they cannot stop us,

    we slide on in, a half a dozen human beings

with the day

    off. Their faces are huge.

Back there someone laughs longer than before, too long.

    Click of prongs against a metal bowl.

And you, you have to take this as I

    give it, don't you, eyes, mouth?

Breathe, friend,

    the *sense* here between us must be gotten past, quick,

as any stalk must be gotten past, any body,

    that the hollowness it ferries up slip into here, quick,

using shape as its cover,

    one of me here and one of me there and in between

this thing, watery,

    like a neck rising and craning out

(wanting so to be seen) (as if there were some other place dear god)—.

When I caught up with them they were down by the pond,
father with X.
I looked into the water where it was stillest.
Saw how each side wants the other to rip it open.
Later that day mother came up into the bathroom,
daylight toothy by then,
color of gunsheen—dusk—

We sat there awhile, neither reached for the switch.
It was not the thing we call time which was ticking
softly. *Come here* she said gripping my head hard in her hands,
both of us facing into the mirror.
Then they struck out into the forest one here one there
wherever they saw it thickest wherever path or track

was absent. As if there were some other place dear god.

Have you ever looked into standing water and seen it going

very fast,
seen the breaks in the image where the suction shows,
where the underneath is pointed and its tip shows through,
maybe something broken, maybe something spoked in there,
your eyes weeds, mouth weeds,
no bed showing through, no pressure from some shore, no

shore? I looked in there.
I thought "I should go in". I thought "I want the fate
to come up now, make it come quick, this thing that is

the predicate"—"is is is" I thought.
The face stayed there.

She put her hand out to the glass.
We both stared in—me in the front of her.
She pulled my hair back very tight.
Took black and started in on the right eye.
Put it on swiftly. Her hands smelled like wine.
She shadowed the cheek, held the lips open, fixed the
edge red. She powdered, streaked. I

never moved. Both of our eyes on the face, on
the third
party.
Reds, blacks.
The light started to go we didn't move.
The silver was gone. The edges on things. The face still glowed—

bright in the wetness, there.
Why should the shut thing not be true enough
anymore?
(*Open up open open* the stillness shrieked.)
Why do we *think*? What is the thinking for?
When Psyche met the god he came down to her

through the opening which is *waiting*,
the *not living* you can keep alive in you,
the god in the house. We painted that alive,
mother with her hands
fixing the outline clear—eyeholes, mouthhole—
forcing the expression on.
Until it was the only thing in the end of the day that seemed

believable,

    and the issue of candor coming awake, there,

one face behind the other peering in,

    and the issue of

freedom. . . .

    Outside it's almost spring in earnest. The Princess

known as *Luciana*

    back from the picnic

has spent one afternoon of light on the lawn tweezing hair

    from her legs. More drinks. The women talk.

Should she marry the arms merchant named Rudi?

    Is hisses the last light on the reddish berries, *is is* the much

blacker shadows of spring now that the leaves are

    opening, now that they're taking up

place.

WHAT IS CALLED THINKING

When I surprised the deer the wind was against me.
So I was given a length
　　of naive time, green time, free,
to be the sole
　　witness,
her blinking in and out of the one ray of light
　　　sorting tufts,
me in the Walkman where the self-reflexive strings of the
　　　　　　　　　eighteenth century
do not die down.
　　I stood there, fast.
Wanted the arabesques of strings, the nervousness, to brand
　　　　　　　　　themselves hard,
　　onto her intangible
pelt. Watched the skin ripple
　　to rid itself of flies. And the ray lacerate
the broad soft back
　　to its infinite pleasure,

and her take a short step through.
　　Up in the air, in the transparent unmoving frenzy, the mind,
oars beat softly in time.
　　A head sank into a gutter (blood starting out).
The strings interpreted (the wind stayed against me).
　　Mother bent to light the candles.
Flight of a bluejay like a struck
　　match.
Then twenty abreast (click) (click).
　　Then twenty abreast marching through the city—

and all along the strings, the strings, bawdy, winged,

    (trying to make sure it's a *story* after

all) . . .

    Barehanded they grip the oars.

The lower limb of the aspen shakes.

    She looks up—it is a she?—

and there is the angel sitting on the limb now.

    There is the angel laughing, sharpening blades.

There is the angel—its robes the *mistakes*

    slapping the taller grasses; its sharpening (the *good*

ideas)—forwards, forwards, forwards, forwards.

    She goes back to feeding, the angel is on her.

He is grinning and slicing the air all round him.

    He is testing the blade (the air is blue).

When I look again it's an AK-47 then it's a saber.

    Look it's a spinning wheel, a printing press—no

it's a run of celluloid in his right hand—he's waving it—

    it's 78 frames of some story—then it's the simple

blade again.

    How can the deer let him ride her?

The *click* is my tape going into

    reverse play. The oboe. The *thinking it's for*

something—that sadness—

    sluffing over the god: tree deer blade:

is it going to braid them up right this time—the good

    elegy—the being

so sorry?

    If I could whip her with the strings,

if I could stab her with the rising sound of

violins—

    but the oars continue above us—we are so small—
and the angel is floating above,

    and the angel is knifing himself
to make the laughter flow

    (although it's breeze-rustle in the honeyed aspen),
over and over the long blade

    going into the windy robes,

sometimes crossing through sometimes staying inside awhile,

    sometimes straight through the throat, then up the nose,
his foliate windiness laughing,

    lacerating the stillness with the silent laughter
(as the breeze picks up down to the left)

    (and she looks up, peering out) and the wind

    begins to change her way,
the angel wild now on the grasses,

    the tree above her wholly hung with knives—hundreds—

                         clacking—
until I want them all to

    fall on her at once—dozens,
into the lowered neck, the saddle—

    the wind changing round altogether now—
until he gives it to me—the good angel—since I

    thought of it: and she turns to

me here now,

and all the blades fall suddenly
into all parts of me giving me my
    human
shape.

History!
    A dress rustles on the spiral staircase.
I lay my forehead into the silver hands.

HISTORY

So that I had to look up just now to see them
sinking—black storks—
  sky disappearing as they ease down,
each body like a prey the wings have seized . . .
  Something that was a *whole story* once,
unparaphrased by shadow,

  something that was the whole cloth floating in a wide
sky,
  rippling, studded with wingbeats,
something like light grazing on the back of light,

  now getting sucked back down
into the watching eye, flapping, black
    hysterical applause,
claws out now looking for foothold,
    high-pitched shrieks,

then many black lowerings—dozens—
  shadowing the empty limbs, the ground,
tripling the shadowload . . .
  Look up and something's unwrapping—
Look up and it's suitors, applause,
  it's fast-forward into the labyrinth,

  smell of ammonia,
lassitude,
  till finally they're settling, shadows of shadows, over
                    the crown, in every

requisite spot.

    Knowledge.

They sit there. Ruffling. The tree is black.

    Should I move? Perhaps they have forgotten me.

Perhaps it is *absolutely true* this thing in the tree

                          above me?

    Perhaps as they hang on hang on it is *the afternoon*?

Voice of what. Seems to say what.

    This is newness? This is the messenger? Screeching.

Clucking.

    Under the frozen river the other river flows

on its side in the dark

    now that it cannot take into itself

the faces, the eyes—the gleam in them—the tossed-up hand

    pointing then casting the pebble

in.

    Forget what we used to be, doubled, in the dark

age where half of us is cast

    in and down, all the way,

into the silt,

    roiled under,

saved in there with all the other slaughtered bits,

    dark thick fabric of the underneath,

sinking, sifting.

    It is four o'clock. I have an appointment.

The tree above me. The river not flowing. Now:

feel the creature, the x:

    me notched into place here,

the grassy riverbank and every individual stem,

    the stalks and seedheads rattling at waterline,

the river made of the eyes of beavers, otters,

    of everything inside watching and listening,

the dredger parked in the river-house,

    the slap slap and click inside the water

the water swallows,

my looking-up, the spine of

    the x—the supple, beastly

spine.

    As long as I stand here, as long as I can stay still,

the x is alive.

    Being here and then the feeling of being. . . .

Everything has its moment.

    The x gnaws on its bone.

When it's time it will know.

    Some part of it bleats, some part of it is

the front, has a face,

when it's time it will be time.

    God it is in no hurry, there is no hurry.

It gnaws on the bone making minutes.

    Let's move

—but it does not move—

    When it's time it will be done,

but it is not time.

    I who used to be inconsolable (and the world

wild around me)

    can stand here now.

It's not that I am alone or that you are or why—

    It's not that we are watched-over or that the x's back

is turned.

    No.

It's that we've grown—

    it's that one must grow—consolable. Listen:

the x gnaws, making stories like small smacking

sounds,

    whole long stories which are its gentle gnawing.

Sometimes it turns onto its side.

    It takes its time.

Let it be so. Shame. Drops of light.

    If the x is on a chain, licking its bone,

making the sounds now of monks

    copying the texts out,

muttering to themselves,

    if it is on a chain

(the lights snapping on now all along the river)

    if it is on a chain

that hisses as it moves with the moving x,

    link by link with the turning x

(the gnawing now Europe burning)

    (the delicate chewing where the atom splits),

if it is on a chain—

    even this beast—even this the favorite beast—

then this is the chain, the gleaming

    chain: that what I wanted was to have looked up at the right

time,

    to see what I was meant to see,

to be pried up out of my immortal soul,

up, into the sizzling quick—

That what I wanted was to have looked up at the only
    right time, the intended time,
punctual,
    the millisecond I was bred to look up into, click, no
half-tone, no orchard of
    possibilities,

up into the eyes of my own
    fate not the world's.
The bough still shakes.

THE PHASE AFTER HISTORY

1

Then two juncos trapped in the house this morning.

    The house like a head with nothing inside.

The voice says: come in.

    The voice always whispering *come in, come.*

Stuck on its one track.

    As if there were only one track.

Only one way in.

    Only one *in.*

The house like a head with nothing inside.

    A table in the white room.

Scissors on the table.

    Two juncos flying desperately around the

room of the house like a head

    (with nothing inside)

the voice-over keeping on (come in, *in*),

    them fizzing around the diagram that makes no

    sense—garden of upstairs and downstairs—wilderness

of materialized

    meaning.

Home.

    Like this piece of paper—

yes take this piece of paper—

    the map of the house like a head with

whatever inside—two birds—

and on it all my efforts to get the *house* out of their
way—
    to make detail withdraw its hot hand,
its competing naturalness—
    Then I open the two doors to make a draft
(here)—
    meaning by that an imbalance

    for them to find and ride—
the inaudible hiss—justice—washing through,
    the white sentence that comes alive to
rectify imbalance—
    —give me a minute.
In the meantime

    they fly into the panes of glass: bright light,
silently they throw themselves into its law: bright light,
    they float past dreamed-up on the screen
called 7 a.m., nesting season, black blurry terms,
    the thwacking of their
heads onto resistant
    surfaces.
Then one escapes,

sucked out by the doorful of sky,
    the insanity, *elsewhere,*
so that—give me a second—
    I no longer remember it,
and the other one vanishes though into here, upstairs,
    the voice still hissing under the track *in in,*

the voice still hissing over the track.
    What you do now is wait

for the sound of wings to be heard
    somewhere in the house
—the *peep* as of glass bottles clinking,
    the lisp of a left-open book read by breeze,
or a hand going into the pile of dead leaves—

(as where there is no *in*, therefore)
    (as where—give me a minute—someone laughs upstairs
but it's really wings
    rustling up there
on the cold current called history
    which means of course it's late and I've
got things

to do).
    How late is it: for instance, is this a sign?
Two birds then one: is it a meaning?
    I start with the attic, moving down.
Once I find it in the guest-
    bedroom but can't
catch it in time,

talking to it all along, hissing: stay there, don't

move—absolutely no
    story—sure there is a sound I could make with my throat
and its cupful of wind that could transmit
    meaning. *Still* I say sharply as I move towards it hands out—
High-pitched the sound it makes with its throat,
    low and too tender the sound it makes with its

    body—against the walls now,

down.

    Which America is it in?

Which America are we in here?

    Is there an America comprised wholly

of its waiting and my waiting and all forms of the thing

even the green's—

    a large uncut fabric floating above the soil—

a place of *attention*?

    The voice says wait. Taking a lot of words.

The voice always says wait.

    The sentence like a tongue

in a higher mouth

    to make the other utterance, the inaudible one,

possible,

    the sentence in its hole, its cavity

of listening,

    flapping, half dead on the wing, through the

hollow indoors,

    the house like a head

with nothing inside

    except this breeze—

shall we keep going?

    Where is it, in the century clicking by?

Where, in the America that *exists*?

    This castle hath a pleasant seat,

the air nimbly recommends itself,

    the guest approves

by his beloved mansionry

    that heaven's breath smells wooingly here.

2

The police came and got Stuart, brought him to
Psych Hospital.

    The face on him the face he'd tried to cut off.
Starting at the edge where the hair is fastened.

    Down behind the ear.
As if to lift it off and give it back. Easy. Something
    gelatinous,
an exterior
    destroyed by mismanagement.

Nonetheless it stayed on.

    You suffer and find the outline, the right
seam (what the suffering is for)—

    you find *where it comes off*: why can't it come off?
The police brought him to Admitting and he can
    be found there.

Who would have imagined a face
    could be so full of blood.

Later he can be found in a room on 4.

    He looks up when you walk in but not at yours.
Hope is something which lies flat against the wall,
    a bad paint job, peeling in spots.
Some people move by in the hallway,

    some are referred elsewhere or they
wait.

    There is a transaction going on up ahead, a commotion.
Shelley is screaming about the Princess.

    There is a draft here but between two unseen

openings.

    And there is the Western God afraid His face would come off
into our eyes

    so that we have to wait in the cleft
rock—remember?—

    His hand still down on it, we're waiting for Him to
go by,

    the back of Him is hope, remember,
the off-white wall,

    the thing-in-us-which-is-a-kind-of-fire fluttering
as we wait in here

    for His hand to lift off,
the thing-in-us-which-is-a-kind-of-air

    getting coated with waiting, with the cold satinfinish,

the thing-which-trails-behind (I dare do all that may

    become a man,
who dares do more is none)

    getting coated, thickly. Oh screw thy story to the
sticking place—

    When he looks up

    because he has had the electric shock,
and maybe even the insulin shock we're not sure,

    the face is gone.
It's hiding somewhere in here now.

    I look and there's no listening in it, foggy place.
We called him the little twinkler

    says his mother at the commitment hearing,

because he was the happiest.

    The blood in the upstairs of the duplex getting cold.

Then we have to get the car unimpounded.

    Send the keys to his parents.

Do they want the car?

    His wrists tied down to the sides of the bed.

And the face on that shouldn't come off.

    The face on that mustn't come off.

Scars all round it along the hairline under the
    chin.

Later he had to take the whole body off

to get the face.

    But me in there while he was still breathing,

both of us waiting to hear something rustle

    and get to it

before it rammed its lights out

    aiming for the brightest spot, the only clue.

Because it is the face

    which must be taken off—?

the forward-pointing of it, history?

    that we be returned to the faceless

attention,

    the waiting and waiting for the telling sound.

Am I alone here?

    Did it get out when the other one did

and I miss it?

    Tomorrow and tomorrow and tomorrow.

The head empty, yes,

    but on it the face, the idea of principal witness,

the long corridor behind it—

    a garden at one end and a garden at

the other—

    the spot of the face

on the expanse of the body,

    the spot on the emptiness (tomorrow and tomorrow),

the spot pointing

    into every direction, looking, trying to find

corners—

(and all along the cloth of Being fluttering)

    (and all along the cloth, the sleep—

before the beginning, before the itch—)

    How I would get it back

sitting here on the second-floor landing,

    one flight above me one flight below,

listening for the one notch

    on the listening which isn't me

listening—

    Sleep, sleep, but on it the dream of reason, eyed,

pointing forward, tapering for entry,

    the *look* with its meeting place at

vanishing point, blade honed for

    quick entry,

etcetera, glance, glance again,

    (make my keen knife see not the

wound it makes)—

    So that you 1) must kill the King—yes—

2) must let her change, change—until you lose her,

    the creature made of nets,

    whose eyes are closed,

whose left hand is raised

    (now now now now hisses the voice)

(her hair made of sentences) and

    3) something new come in but

what? listening.

    Is the house empty?

Is the emptiness housed?

    Where is America here from the landing, my face on

my knees, eyes closed to hear

    further?

Lady M. is the intermediary phase.

    God help us.

Unsexed unmanned.

    Her open hand like a verb slowly descending onto

                            the free,

her open hand fluttering all round her face now,

    trying to still her gaze, to snag it on

those white hands waving and diving

    in the water that is not there.

SOUL SAYS

(Afterword)

To be so held by brittleness, shapeliness.
By meaning. As where I *have to go where you go*,
I *have to touch what you must touch*,
in hunger, in boredom, the spindrift, the ticket . . .
Distilled in you (can you hear me)
the idiom in you, the why—

The flash *of a voice*. The river *glints*.
The mother *opens the tablecloth up into the wind*.
There as the fabric descends—the alphabet of ripenesses,
what is, what could have been.
The bread on the tablecloth. Crickets shrill in the grass.

O pluck my magic garment from me. So.
                              [lays down his robe]
Lie there, my art—

(This is a form of matter of matter she sang)

(Where the hurry is stopped) (and held) (but not extinguished) (no)

(So listen, listen, this will soothe you) (if that is what you want)

Now then, I said, I go to meet that which I liken to
(even though the wave break and drown me in laughter)
the wave breaking, the wave drowning me in laughter—

from

MATERIALISM

THE SURFACE

It has a hole in it. Not only where I
        concentrate.
The river still ribboning, twisting up,
        into its re-
arrangements, chill enlightenments, tight-knotted
        quickenings
and loosenings—whispered messages dissolving
        the messengers—
the river still glinting-up into its handfuls, heapings,
        glassy
forgettings under the river of
my attention—
and the river of my attention laying itself down—
        bending,
reassembling—over the quick leaving-offs and windy
        obstacles—
and the surface rippling under the wind's attention—
rippling over the accumulations, the slowed-down drifting
        permanences
of the cold
bed.
I say *iridescent* and I look down.
The leaves very still as they are carried.

NOTES ON THE REALITY OF THE SELF

Watching the river, each handful of it closing over the next,

brown and swollen. Oaklimbs,

gnawed at by waterfilm, lifted, relifted, lapped-at all day in

this dance of non-discovery. All things are

possible. Last year's leaves, coming unstuck from shore,

rippling suddenly again with the illusion,

and carried, twirling, shiny again and fat,

towards the quick throes of another tentative

conclusion, bobbing, circling in little suctions their stiff

                                            presence

on the surface compels. Nothing is virtual.

The long brown throat of it sucking up from some faraway melt.

Expression pouring forth, all content no meaning.

The force of it and the thingness of it identical.

Spit forth, licked up, snapped where the force

exceeds the weight, clickings, pockets.

A long sigh through the land, an exhalation.

I let the dog loose in this stretch. Crocus

appear in the gassy dank leaves. Many

earth gasses, rot gasses.

I take them in, breath at a time. I put my

breath back out

onto the scented immaterial. How the invisible

roils. I see it from here and then

I see it from here. Is there a new way of looking—

valences and little hooks—inevitabilities, proba-

bilities? It flaps and slaps. Is this body the one

I know as me? How private these words? And these? Can you

smell it, brown with little froths at the rot's lips,

meanwhiles and meanwhiles thawing then growing soggy then

the filaments where leaf-matter accrued round a

pattern, a law, slipping off, precariously, bit by bit,

and flicks, and swiftnesses suddenly more water than not.

The nature of goodness the mind exhales.

I see myself. I am a widening angle of

and *nevertheless* and *this performance has rapidly*—

nailing each point and then each next right point, inter-

locking, correct, correct again, each rightness snapping loose,

floating, hook in the air, swirling, seed-down,

quick—*the evidence of the visual henceforth*—and henceforth, loosening—

NOTES ON THE REALITY OF THE SELF

In my bushes facing the bandpractice field,

in the last light, surrounded by drumbeats, drumrolls,

there is a wind that tips the reddish leaves

exactly all one way, seizing them up from underneath, making them

barbarous in unison. Meanwhile the light insists they glow

where the wind churns, or, no, there is a wide gold corridor

of thick insistent light, layered with golds, as if runged,

as if laid low from the edge of the sky,

in and out of which the coupling and uncoupling

limbs—the racks of limbs—the luminosities of branchings—

offspring and more offspring—roil—(except when a sudden

                                 stillness reveals

an appal of pure form, pure light—

every rim clear, every leaf serrated, tongued—stripped

of the gauzy quicknesses which seemed its flesh)—but then

                               the instabilities

regroup, and the upper limbs of the tall oaks

begin to whine again with wide slappings

which seep ever-downward to my bushes—into them, through them—

to where the very grass makes congress with the busyness—

mutating, ridging, threshing this light from that, to no

avail—and in it all

the drumroll, rising as the ranks join in,

the wild branches letting the even drumbeats through,

ripples let through as the red branches spiral, tease,

as the crescendos of the single master-drummer

rise, and birds scatter over the field, and the wind makes each

                                   thing

kneel and rise, kneel and rise, never-ending stringy

almost maternal lurching of wind

pushing into and out of the russets, magentas, incarnadines . . .

Tell me, where are the drumbeats which fully load and expand

each second,

bloating it up, cell-like, making it real, where are they

to go, what will *they* fill up

pouring forth, pouring round the subaqueous magenta bushes

which dagger the wind back down on itself,

tenderly, prudently, almost loaded down

with regret? For there is not a sound the bushes will take

from the multitude beyond them, in the field, uniformed—

(all left now on one heel) (right) (all fifty trumpets up

to the sun)—not a molecule of sound

from the tactics of this glistening beast,

forelimbs of silver (trombones, french horns)

(anointed by the day itself) expanding, retracting,

bits of red from the surrounding foliage deep

in all the fulgid

instruments—orient—ablaze where the sound is released—

trumpeting, unfolding—

screeching, rolling, patterning, measuring—

scintillant beast the bushes do not know exists

as the wind beats them, beats in them, beats round them,

them in a wind that does not really even now

exist,

in which these knobby reddish limbs that do not sway

by so much as an inch

its arctic course

themselves now sway—

THE DREAM OF THE UNIFIED FIELD

1

On my way to bringing you the leotard
you forgot to include in your overnight bag,
the snow started coming down harder.
I watched each gathering of leafy flakes
melt round my footfall.
I looked up into it—late afternoon but bright.
Nothing true or false in itself. Just motion. Many strips of
motion. Filaments of falling marked by the tiny certainties
of flakes. Never blurring yet themselves a cloud. Me in it

          and yet

moving easily through it, black lycra leotard balled into

          my pocket,

your tiny dream in it, my left hand on it or in it

          to keep

warm. Praise this. Praise that. Flash a glance up and try

          to see

the arabesques and runnels, gathering and loosening, as they
define, as a voice would, the passaging through from

          the-other-than-

human. Gone as they hit the earth. But embellishing.
Flourishing. The road with me on it going on through. In-
scribed with the present. As if it really
were possible to exist, and exist, never to be pulled back
in, given and given never to be received. The music
of the footfalls doesn't stop, doesn't
mean. *Here are your things*, I said.

Starting home I heard—bothering, lifting, then
                              bothering again—
the huge flock of starlings massed over our
                    neighborhood
these days; heard them lift and
swim overhead through the falling snow
as though the austerity of a true, cold thing, a verity,
the black bits of their thousands of bodies swarming
                                        then settling
overhead. I stopped. All up and down the empty oak
they stilled. Every limb sprouting. Every leafy backlit
                                        body
filling its part of the empty crown. I tried to count—
then tried to estimate—
but the leaves of this wet black tree at the heart of
                    the storm—shiny—
river through limbs, back onto the limbs,
scatter, blow away, scatter, recollect—
undoing again and again the tree without it ever ceasing to be
                                              full.
Foliage of the tree of the world's waiting.
Of having waited a long time and
                    still having
to wait. Of trailing and screaming.
Of engulfed readjustments. Of blackness redisappearing
                                        into
downdrafts of snow. Of indifference. Of indifferent
                    reappearings.
                    I think of you
back of me now in the bright house of
                    your friend

twirling in the living room in the shiny leotard
                              you love.
I had looked—as I was leaving—through the window
to see you, slick in your magic,
pulling away from the wall—

I watch the head explode then recollect, explode, recollect.

                              3

Then I heard it, inside the swarm, the single cry

of the crow. One syllable—one—inside the screeching and the
                                        skittering,
inside the constant repatterning of a thing not nervous yet
                              not ever
still—but not uncertain—without obedience
yet not without law—one syllable—
black, shiny, twirling on its single stem,
rooting, one foot on the earth,
twisting and twisting—

and then again—a little further off this time—*down the
ravine*, a voice inside a head, filling a head. . . .

See, my pocket is empty now. I let my hand
open and shut in there. I do it again. Two now, skull and
                              pocket
with their terrified inhabitants.

You turn the music up. The window nothing to you, liquid, dark,
where now your mother has come back to watch.

Closeup, he's blue—streaked iris blue, india-ink blue—and
black—an oily, fiery set of blacks—none of them
true—as where hate and order touch—something that cannot
become known. Stages of black but without
graduation. So there is no direction.
All of this happened, yes. Then disappeared
into the body of the crow, chorus of meanings,
layers of blacks, then just the crow, plain, big,
lifting his claws to walk thrustingly
forward and back—indigo, cyanine, beryl, grape, steel . . . Then suddenly he
wings and—braking as he lifts
the chest in which an eye-sized heart now beats—
—he's up—a blunt clean stroke—
one ink-streak on the early evening snowlit scene—
See the gesture of the painter?—Recall the
crow?—Place him quickly on his limb as he comes sheering in,
close to the trunk, to land—Is he now
disappeared again?

. . . .*long neck, up, up with the head,*
eyes on the fingertips, bent leg, shift of
the weight—*turn*—No, no, begin again . . .
What had she seen, Madame Sakaroff, at Stalingrad, now in
her room of mirrors tapping her cane
as the piano player begins the interrupted Minuet again
and we line up right foot extended, right
hand extended, the Bach mid-phrase—
Europe? The dream of Europe?—midwinter afternoon,
rain at the windowpane, ceilings at thirty feet and coffered

floating over the wide interior spaces . . .

No one must believe in God again I heard her say

one time when I had come to class too soon

and had been sent to change. The visitor had left,

kissing her hand, small bow, and I had seen her (from the curtain)

(having forgotten I was there)

turn from the huge pearl-inlaid doors she had just closed,

one hand still on the massive, gold, bird-headed knob,

and see—a hundred feet away—herself—a woman in black in

       a mirrored room—

saw her not shift her gaze but bring her pallid tensile hand—

as if it were not part of her—slowly down from

the ridged, cold, feathered knob and, recollected, fixed upon

      that other woman, emigrée,

begin to move in stiffly towards her . . . You out there

         now,

you in here with me—I watched the two of them,

black and black, in the gigantic light,

glide at each other, heads raised, necks long—

me wanting to cry out—where were the others?—wasn't it late?

the two of her like huge black hands—

clap once and once only and the signal is given—

but to what?—regarding what?—till closer-in I saw

      more suddenly

how her eyes eyed themselves: no wavering:

like a vast silver page burning: the black hole

      expanding:

like a meaning coming up quick from inside that page—

coming up quick to seize the reading face—

each face wanting the other to *take* it—

but where? and *from* where?—I was eight—

I saw the different weights of things,

saw the vivid performance of the present,

156

saw the light rippling almost shuddering where her body finally

touched

the image, the silver film between them like something that would have

shed itself in nature now

but wouldn't, couldn't, here, on tight,

between, not thinning, not slipping off to let some

seed-down

through, no signal in it, no information . . . Child,

what should I know

to save you that I do not know, hands on this windowpane?—

6

The storm: I close my eyes and,

standing in it, try to make it *mine*. An inside

thing. Once I was. . . . once, once.

It settles, in my head, the wavering white

sleep, the instances—they stick, accrue,

grip up, connect, they do not melt,

I will not let them melt, they build, cloud and cloud,

I feel myself weak, I feel the thinking muscle-up—

outside, the talk-talk of the birds—outside,

strings and their roots, leaves inside the limbs,

in some spots the skin breaking—

but inside, no more exploding, no more smoldering, no more,

inside, a splinter colony, new world, possession

gripping down to form,

wilderness brought deep into my clearing,

out of the ooze of night,

limbed, shouldered, necked, visaged, the white—

now the clouds coming in (don't look up),

now the Age behind the clouds, The Great Heights,

all in there, reclining, eyes closed, huge,

centuries and centuries long and wide,

and underneath, barely attached but attached,

like a runner, my body, my tiny piece of

the century—minutes, houses going by—The Great

Heights—

anchored by these footsteps, now and now,

the footstepping—now and now—carrying its vast

white sleeping geography—mapped—

not a lease—*possession*—"At the hour of vespers

in a sudden blinding snow,

they entered the harbor and he named it Puerto de

7

San Nicolás and at its entrance he imagined he

could see

its beauty and goodness, *sand right up to the land*

where you can put the side of a ship. He thought

he saw

Indians fleeing through the white before

the ship . . . As for him, he did not believe what his

crew

told him, nor did he understand them well, nor they

him. In the white swirl, he placed a large cross

at the western side of

the harbor, on a conspicuous height,

as a sign that Your Highness claim the land as

Your own. After the cross was set up,

three sailors went into the bush (immediately erased

from sight by the fast snow) to see what kinds of

trees. They captured three very black Indian

women—one who was young and pretty.

The Admiral ordered her clothed and returned her to

her land

courteously. There her people told

she had not wanted to leave the ship,

but wished to stay on it. The snow was wild.

Inside it, though, you could see

this woman was wearing a little piece of

gold on her nose, which was a sign there was

gold

in that land"—

OPULENCE

The self-brewing of the amaryllis rising before me.
Weeks of something's decomposing—like hearsay
growing—into this stringent self-analysis—
a tyranny of utter self-reflexiveness—
its nearness to the invisible a deep fissure
the days suck round as its frontiers trill, slur
—a settling-ever-upward and then,

now,

this utterly sound-free-though-tongued opening
where some immortal scale is screeched—
bits of *clench*, *jolt*, *fray* and *assuage*—
bits of *gnaw* and *pulse* and, even, *ruse*
—impregnable dribble—wingbeat at a speed
too slow to see—stepping out of the casing outstretched,

high-heeled—

something from underneath coaxing the packed buds up,
loosening their perfect fit—the smooth skin between them

striating then

beginning to wrinkle and fold
so as to loosen the tight dictation of the four inseparable polished

and bullioned

buds—color seeping up till the icy green releases the sensation of

a set of reds

imprisoned in it, flushed, though not yet truly
visible—the green still starchy—clean—
till the four knots grow loose in their armor,

and the two dimensions of their perfect-fit fill out, and a third,

shadow, seeps in

loosening and loosening,

and the envelope rips,

and the fringes slip off and begin to fray at their newly freed tips,

and the enameled, vaulting, perfectly braided

immaculate

is jostled, unpacked—

the force, the phantom, now sending armloads up

into the exclamation,

and the skin marbles, and then, when I look again,

has already begun to speckle, then blush, then a solid un-

avoidable incarnadine,

the fourness of it now maneuvering, vitalized,

like antennae rearranging constantly,

the monologue reduced—or is it expanded—to

this chatter seeking all the bits of light,

the four of them craning this way then that according to

the time

of day, the drying wrinkled skirts of the casing

now folded-down beneath, formulaic,

the light wide-awake around it—or is it the eye—

yes yes yes yes says the mechanism of the underneath tick tock—

and no footprints to or from the place—

no footprints to or from—

THE VISIBLE WORLD

I dig my hands into the absolute. The surface
                              breaks
into shingled, grassed clusters; lifts.
If I press, pick-in with fingers, pluck,
I can unfold the loam. It is tender. It is a tender
maneuver, hands making and unmaking promises.
Diggers, forgetters. . . . A series of successive single instances . . .
Frames of reference moving . . .
The speed of light, down here, upthrown, in my hands:
bacteria, milky roots, pilgrimages of spores, deranged
                              and rippling
mosses. What heat is this in me
that would *thaw time*, making bits of instance
                              overlap
shovel by shovelful—my present a wind blowing through
                              this culture
slogged and clutched-firm with decisions, over-ridings,
                              opportunities
taken? . . . If I look carefully, there in my hand, if I
                    break it apart without
crumbling: husks, mossy beginnings and endings, ruffled
                              airy loam-bits,
and the greasy silks of clay crushing the pinerot
                              in . . .
Erasure. Tell me something and then take it back.
Bring this pellucid moment—here on this page now
                    as on this patch

of soil, my property—bring it up to the top and out
                                                    of
sequence. Make it dumb again—won't you?—what
                                        would it
take? Leach the humidities out, the things that will
                                        insist on
making meaning. Parch it. It isn't hard: just take this
                                        shovelful
and spread it out, deranged, a vertigo of single
                                        clots
in full sun and you can, easy, decivilize it, un-
                                        hinge it
from its plot. Upthrown like this, I think you can
                                        eventually
abstract it. Do you wish to?
Disentangled, it grows very very clear.
Even the mud, the sticky lemon-colored clay
hardens and then yields, crumbs.
I can't say what it is then, but the golden-headed
                                        hallucination,
mating, forgetting, speckling, inter-
                        locking,
will begin to be gone from it and then its glamorous
                                        veil of
echoes and muddy nostalgias will
be gone. If I touch the slender new rootings they show me
                                        how large I
am, look at these fingers—what a pilot—I touch, I press
                                        their slowest
electricity. . . . What speed is it at?
What speed am I at here, on my knees, as the sun traverses now
                                        and just begins

to touch my back. What speed where my fingers, under the

dark oaks,

are suddenly touched, lit up—so white as they move, the ray for

a moment

on them alone in the small wood.

White hands in the black-green glade,

opening the muddy cartoon of the present, taking the tiny roots

of the moss

apart, hired hands, curiosity's small army, so white

in these greens—

make your revolution in the invisible temple,

make your temple in the invisible

revolution—I can't see the errands you run, hands gleaming

for this instant longer

like tinfoil at the bottom here of the tall

whispering oaks . . .

Listen, Boccioni the futurist says a galloping horse

has not four

legs (it has twenty)—and "at C there is no sequence

because there is no time"—and since

at lightspeed, etc. (everything is simultaneous): my hands

serrated with desires, shoved into these excavated

fates

—mauve, maroons, gutters of flecking golds—

my hands are living in myriad manifestations

of light. . . .

"All forms of imitation are to be despised."

"All subjects previously used must be discarded."

"At last we shall rush rapidly past objectiveness" . . .

Oh enslavement will you take these hands

and hold them in

for a time longer? Tops of the oaks, do you see my tiny

                                        golden hands

pushed, up to the wrists,

into the present? Star I can't see in daylight, young, light

                                      and airy star—

I put the seed in. The beam moves on.

from

THE ERRANCY

THE GUARDIAN ANGEL OF THE LITTLE UTOPIA

Shall I move the flowers again?
Shall I put them further to the left
into the light?
Will that fix it, will that arrange the
thing?
Yellow sky.
Faint cricket in the dried-out bush.
As I approach, my footfall in the leaves
drowns out the cricket-chirping I was
coming close to hear . . .
Yellow sky with black leaves rearranging it.
Wind rearranging the black leaves in it.
But anyway I am indoors, of course, and this is a pane, here,
and I have arranged the flowers for you
again. Have taken the dead cordless ones, the yellow bits past apogee,
the faded cloth, the pollen-free abandoned marriage-hymn
back out, leaving the few crisp blooms to swagger, winglets, limpid
                                     debris. . . .

Shall I arrange these few remaining flowers?
Shall I rearrange these gossamer efficiencies?
Please don't touch me with your skin.
Please let the thing evaporate.
Please tell me clearly what it is.
The party is so loud downstairs, bristling with souvenirs.
It's a philosophy of life, of course,
drinks fluorescent, whips of syntax in the air
above the heads—how small they seem from here,

the bobbing universal heads, stuffing the void with eloquence,
and also tiny merciless darts
of truth. It's pulled on tight, the air they breathe and rip.
It's like a prize the way it's stretched on tight
over the voices, keeping them intermingling, forcing the breaths to
marry, marry,
cunning little hermeneutic cupola,
dome of occasion in which the thoughts re-
group, the footprints stall and gnaw in tiny ruts,
the napkins wave, are waved, the honeycombing
thoughts are felt to *dialogue,* a form of self-
congratulation, no?, or is it suffering? I'm a bit
dizzy up here rearranging things,
they will come up here soon, and need a setting for their fears,
and loves, an architecture for their evolutionary
morphic needs—what will they *need* if I don't make the place?—
what will they know to miss?, what cry out for, what feel the bitter
restless irritations
for? A bit dizzy from the altitude of everlastingness,
the tireless altitudes of the created place,
in which to make a life—a *liberty*—the hollow, fetishized, and starry
place,
a bit gossamer with dream, a vortex of evaporations,
oh little dream, invisible city, invisible hill
I make here on the upper floors for you—
down there, where you are entertained, where you are passing
time, there's glass and moss on air,
there's the feeling of being numerous, mouths submitting to air, lips
to protocol,
and dreams of sense, tongues, hinges, forceps clicking
in anticipation of . . . as if the moment, freeze-burned by accuracies-of
could be thawed open into life again
by gladnesses, by rectitude—no, no—by the sinewy efforts at

sincerity—can't you feel it gliding round you,

mutating, yielding the effort-filled phrases of your talk to air,

compounding, stemming them, honeying-open the sheerest

                                        innuendoes till

the rightness seems to root, in the air, in the compact indoor sky,

and the rest, all round, feels like desert, falls away,

and you have the sensation of muscular timeliness,

and you feel the calligraphic in you reach out like a soul

into the midst of others, in conversation,

gloved by desire, into the tiny carnage

of opinions. . . . So dizzy. Life buzzing beneath me

though my feeling says the hive is gone, queen gone,

the continuum continuing beneath, busy, earnest, in con-

versation. Shall I prepare. Shall I put this further

to the left, shall I move the light, the point-of-view, the shades are

drawn, to cast a glow resembling disappearance, slightly red,

will that fix it, will that make clear the task, the trellised ongoingness

and all these tiny purposes, these parables, this marketplace

of tightening truths?

Oh knit me that am crumpled dust,

the heap is all dispersed. Knit me that *am*. Say *therefore*. Say

philosophy and mean by that the pane.

Let us look out again. The yellow sky.

With black leaves rearranging it. . . .

THE SCANNING

1.

After the rain there was traffic behind us like a long kiss.
The ramp harrowing its mathematics like a newcomer who likes
                                                    the rules—
glint and whir of piloting minds, gripped steering-wheels . . .
Jacob waiting and the angel *didn't show*.
Meanwhile the stations the scanner glides over, not selecting, hiss—
islands the heat-seekers missed
in the large sea of. . . . And after lunch
the long-distance starts up pianissimo—wires glinting where the
                                                    frontage road
parallels the interstate for a little, narrow, while.
Elsewhere, from the air, something *softens* the scape—
which activity precedes, though doesn't necessarily require,
the carpet-bombing that often follows—
And the bands of our listening scan
the bands of static,
seeking a resting point, asymptotic, listening in the hiss
for the hoarse snagged points where meaning seemingly
accrues: three notes: three silences: intake
of breath: turnstile?: a glint in fog?: what the listener
will wait-into, hoping for a place to
stop . . . Jacob waited and the angel didn't—

Once off the interstate, we exhausted the tangible.

The plan seemed to dagger forward on its own, towards the horizon-line,

the future its mother-of-pearl cadaver, down there, where the map

continues

onto the next blue page. . . . *Our* plan.

One must not pretend one knew nothing of it.

One must not pretend one didn't tenderly finger its heavenly style.

The skyline itself, bluing now towards evening,

the spidery picture of the plan we tongued up—

unquenchable—where were you?—never-to-be-defined,

a solo first-fruit performance for which the eye

is still intended. . . . What shall we move with

now that the eye must shut? What shall we sift with

now that the mind must blur? What shall we undress the veilings of

dusk with,

what shall we harvest the nothingness with,

now that the hands must be tucked back in their pockets,

now that the bright shirt of the over-ripe heart

must be taken off and the skin of things restored,

the long-haul restored (where the quicknesses had reigned),

the carpenter arriving as if out of the skyways

with a measure in hand, a sad eye, a vague patience—

the tongue-tied carpenter ready to scribble and strengthen . . .

Our plan . . . To get the beauty of it hot.

The angel called out but Jacob, Jacob . . .

3.

Down by the riverbed I found some geese asleep.

I could see the billboards, but they were across the water.

Maybe two hundred geese—now beginning to stir,

purring and cooing at my walking among them.

Groping their armless way, their underneaths greening.

A slow roiling. As of redundancy. Squirming as they sponge

over the short wet grass—bunchy—the river behind presenting

lapidary

faithfulness—*plink*—

no common motion in the turbaned brooding,

all shoulder and waddle,

foliage darkening to feathers above their vague iridescence . . .

A mess of geese. Unperfectable. A mess

of conflicting notions. Something that doesn't have to be

imagined. An end-zone one can have pushed forward to,

here at the end of the path, what the whole freeway led to,

what the whole adventure led to,

galleys, slaves, log-books,

tiny calculations once it got dark enough to see,

what the whole madness led to—the curiosity—viral—here,

like a sign—thick but clear—here at the bottom of the sedge,

the city still glimmering over there in the distance,

but us here, for no reason, where the mass of geese are rousing,

necessity and circumstance quivering in each other's arms,

us in each other's arms, or, no, not really.

4.

The angel was on the telephone.

No, Jacob was on the telephone.

There was no doorway through which to pass.

For either of them. No flaming gateway. No wafer-thin scribble

to *understand*. . . .

Was it really, then, a pastime, the hostile universe?

Was the wrestling a mental color, an architecture of mockery, a self-portrait of the unmargined thing by the margined thing?

The geese seemed to assemble, the freeway hissed.

Oh to sleep the sleep of those who are alive. . . .

The brain extended its sugared fingertips.

Itching so to create something new.

Slightly, profoundly, the riverbottom gleamed.

5.

Then *here*, and *here*, a freckling of the light,

as where parts curdle up

to fetch a whole—and the birds lift up—

and from the undulant swagger-stabs of peck and wingflap,

collisions and wobbly runs—out of the manyness—

a molting of the singular,

a frenzied search (upflapping, heavy) for cadence, and then

cadence found, a diagram appearing on the air, at arctic heights,

an armoring

the light puts on—stagger of current-flap become unacrobatic industry,

no tremble in it,

no echo—below, the freeway lustrous with accurate intention—

above us now, the sky lustrous with the skeleton of the dream of

reason—look up!—

Jacob dreamer—the winged volumetrics chiseling out a skull

for the dream—

THINKING

I can't really remember now. The soundless foamed.

A crow hung like a cough to a wire above me. There was a chill.

It was a version of a crow, untitled as such, tightly feathered

in the chafing air. Rain was expected. All round him air

dilated, as if my steady glance on him, cindering at the glance-core where

it held him tightest, swelled and sucked,

while round that core, first a transition, granular—then remembrance of

thing being

seen—remembrance as it thins-out into matter, almost listless—then,

sorrow—if sorrow could be sterile—and the rest fraying off into all

the directions,

variegated amnesias—lawns, black panes, screens the daylight

thralls into in search of well-edged things. . . . If I squint, he glints.

The wire he's on wobbly and his grip not firm.

Lifting each forked clawgrip again and again.

Every bit of wind toying with his hive of black balance.

Every now and then a passing car underneath causing a quick rearrangement.

The phonelines from six houses, and the powerlines from three

grouped-up above me—some first-rung of sky—him not comfortable,

nature silted-in to this maximum habitat—*freedom*—

passers-by (woman, dog) vaguely relevant I'd guess though he doesn't

look down,

eyeing all round, disqualifying, disqualifying

all the bits within radius that hold no clue

to whatever is sought, urgent but without hurry,

me still by this hedge now, waiting for his black to blossom,

then wing-thrash where he falls at first against the powerline,

then updraft seized, gravity winnowed, the falling raggedly
reversed, depth suddenly pursued, its invisibility ridged—bless him—
until he is off, hinge by hinge, built of tiny wingtucks, filaments
of flapped-back wind, until the thing (along whose spine
his sentence of black talk, thrashing, wrinkling, dissipates—the history,
                                                    the wiring,

shaking, with light—) is born.

STUDIES IN SECRECY

The secret we don't know we're trying to find, the thing *un-*

seen,

is it ironic? is it a sign of anything?—raw

vertigo

the suction-point of which we now are trying to feed

our lives

into—the point devoid of ancestry, the bullioned point,

so sleek,

dwindling yet increasingly aswarm,

the chittering of manyness in it as it is made to

clot

into a thrumming singleness—the secret—the place where the words

twist—

we are looking for it everywhere—

we look on my breast, we try the nipple,

we look in the gaiety of your fingertips, the curriculum

of caresses

twisting and windy in the architecture of

my neck, my

open mouth—we look in your mouth—

we look, quick, into the-day-before-yesterday—we look

away—

we look again into your violent mouth,

into the edifice of your whisper, into the dwindling oxygen

we eat,

inhaling, exhaling—

we look into the glassy eyes we have between us—

we try not to shift, we stare,

there seems to be an enclosure in there, maybe a struck

> note, an hypothesis,

we look in each other's hair

as in ripe shrubs bearing and withering,

we feel time glide through the room, between our legs,

round through our glance—we think we can look in the walled-up

> thoughts—

we let our nights get tangled, we try to stare—

if something happens—the phone rings, a cigarette is lit,

maybe a massacre, maybe in spring the curtain

blossoms—gossamer—we look in there—

then we go back to the green-eyed heat, and stare,

beating on the icy film between each thing, knocking, tapping,

> to see what's happening,

"the wasteland grows; woe to him hiding wastelands

> within"(*The Portable*

Nietzsche—Viking '54—we look in there),

also look in "Alas, the time is coming when

man will no longer shoot the arrow of his longing

beyond man"—"the string of his bow has forgotten

to whir"—it is a haze—the radio's

> on, the automated

churchbells ring—we start the matter up again, we cry, we finger

the folds—we open our lips—we bite our necks—

don't make me explain, one wing of it is soot, one wing

> of it is blood,

we lick it, we nibble aimlessly, not so much tired as

increasingly ignorant—the minutes barbed now—the

blue streak where we hear a siren louder now,

our shoulders glistening, our backs greasy with hope,

foraging now (we try the book again) (we try putting things

> in each other

to see how much room)("the earth has become smaller

and on it hop

the last men") so that we have to start

saying the words again (the last men live longest)—

I love you I say—poor secret, did you need us?

did you need us to find you?—

(live longest—*we have invented happiness*, they say)—

I love you, you say, rising among the motes, the spores—

and *forever and forever* like a sleeve we slide the hissing secret in—

the golden-headed, the upthrown—have invented *happiness* say the

last men—

and blink.

LE MANTEAU DE PASCAL

I have put on my great coat it is cold.

It is an outer garment.

Coarse, woolen.

Of unknown origin.

∞

It has a fine inner lining but it is
as an exterior that you see it—a grace.

∞

I have a coat I am wearing. It is a fine admixture.
The woman who threw the threads in the two directions, headlong,
has made, skillfully, something dark-true,
as the evening calls the birds up into
the branches of the shaven hedgerows,
to twitter bodily
a makeshift coat—the boxelder cut back stringently by the owner
that more might grow next year, and thicker, you know—
the birds tucked gestures on the inner branches—
and space in the heart,
not shade-giving, not
chronological . . . Oh transformer, logic, where are you here in this fold,

my name being called out now but back, behind,

in the upper world. . . .

∽

I have a coat I am wearing I was told to wear it.

Someone knelt down each morning to button it up.

I looked at their face, down low, near me.

What is *longing?* what is a *star?*

Watched each button a peapod getting tucked back in.

Watched harm with its planeloads folded up in the sleeves.

Watched grappling hooks trawl through the late-night waters.

Watched bands of stations scan unable to ascertain.

There are fingers, friend, that never grow sluggish.

They crawl up the coat and don't miss an eyehole.

Glinting in kitchenlight.

Supervised by the traffic god.

Hissed at by grassblades that wire-up, outside,

their stirring rhetoric—this is your land, this is my *my*—

∽

You do understand, don't you, by looking?

The coat, which is itself a ramification, a city,

floats vulnerably above another city, ours,

the *city on the hill* (only with hill gone),

floats in illustration

of what was once believed, and thus was visible—

(all things believed are visible)—

floats a Jacob's ladder with hovering empty arms, an open throat,

a place where a heart may beat if it wishes,

pockets that hang awaiting the sandy whirr of a small secret, folds where the legs could be, with their kneeling mechanism,

the floating fatigue of an after-dinner herald,

not guilty of any treason towards life except fatigue,

a skillfully-cut coat, without chronology,

filled with the sensation of being suddenly completed—

as then it is, abruptly, the last stitch laid in, the knot bit off—

hung there in gravity, as if its innermost desire,

numberless the awaitings flickering around it,

the other created things also floating but not of the same order, no,

not like this form, built so perfectly to mantle the body,

the neck like a vase awaiting its cut flower,

a skirting barely visible where the tucks indicate

the mild loss of bearing in the small of the back,

the grammar, so strict, of the two exact shoulders—

and the law of the shouldering—

and the chill allowed to skitter-up through,

and those crucial spots where the fit cannot be perfect—

oh skirted loosening aswarm with lessenings,

with the mild pallors of unaccomplishment,

flaps night-air collects in,

folds . . . But the night does not annul its belief in,

the night preserves its love for, this one narrowing of infinity,

that floats up into the royal starpocked blue its ripped, distracted

                                        supervisor—

this coat awaiting recollection,

this coat awaiting the fleeting moment, the true moment, the hill, the

                                        vision of the hill,

and then the moment when the prize is lost, and the erotic tinglings

                                of the dream of reason

are left to linger mildly in the weave of the fabric,

the wool gabardine mix, with its grammatical weave,

never never destined to lose its elasticity,

its openness to abandonment,
its willingness to be disturbed.

∞

July 11 . . . Oaks: the organization of this tree is difficult. Speaking
generally no doubt the determining planes are concentric, a system of
brief contiguous and continuous tangents, whereas those of the cedar
wd. roughly be called horizontals and those of the beech radiating but
modified by droop and by a screw-set towards jutting points. But beyond
this since the normal growth of the boughs is radiating there is a system of
spoke-wise clubs of green—sleeve-pieces. And since the end shoots curl
and carry young scanty leaf-stars these clubs are tapered, and I have seen
also pieces in profile with chiselled outlines, the blocks thus made
detached and lessening towards the end. However the knot-star is the chief
thing: it is whorled, worked round, and this is what keeps up the illusion
of the tree. Oaks differ much, and much turns on the broadness of the
leaves, the narrower giving the crisped and starry and catherine-wheel
forms, the broader the flat-pieced mailed or chard-covered ones, in wh. it
is possible to see composition in dips, etc. But I shall study them further.
It was this night I believe but possibly the next that I saw clearly the
impossibility of staying in the Church of England.

∞

How many coats do you think it will take?

The coat was a great-coat.

The Emperor's coat was.

How many coats do you think it will take?

The undercoat is dry. What we now want is?

The sky can analyze the coat because of the rips in it.

The sky shivers through the coat because of the rips in it.

The rips in the sky ripen through the rips in the coat.

There is no quarrel.

∞

I take off my coat and carry it.

∞

There is no emergency.

∞

I only made that up.

∞

Behind everything the sound of something dripping

The sound of something: I will vanish, others will come here, what is that?

The canvas flapping in the wind like the first notes of our absence

An origin is not an action though it occurs at the very start

Desire goes traveling into the total dark of another's soul

looking for where it breaks off

I was a hard thing to undo

∽

The life of a customer

What came on the paper plate

overheard nearby

an impermanence   of structure

watching the lip-reading

had loved but couldn't now recognize

∽

What are the objects, then, that man should consider most important?

What sort of a question is that he asks them.

The eye only discovers the visible slowly.

It floats before us asking to be worn,

offering "we must think about objects at the very moment
when all their meaning is abandoning them"

and "the title provides a protection from significance"

and "we are responsible for the universe."

∞

I have put on my doubting, my wager, it is cold.

It is an outer garment, or, conversely, a natural covering,

so coarse and woolen, also of unknown origin,

a barely apprehensible dilution of evening into

an outer garment, or, conversely, a natural covering,

to twitter bodily a makeshift coat,

that more might grow next year, and thicker, you know,

not shade-giving, not chronological,

my name being called out now but from out back, behind,

an outer garment, so coarse and woolen,

also of unknown origin, not shade-giving, not chronological,

each harm with its planeloads folded up in the sleeves,

you do understand, don't you, by looking?

the Jacob's ladder with its floating arms its open throat,

that more might grow next year, and thicker, you know,

filled with the sensation of being suddenly completed,

the other created things also floating but not of the same order,

not shade-giving, not chronological,

you do understand, don't you, by looking?

a neck like a vase awaiting its cut flower,

filled with the sensation of being suddenly completed,

the moment the prize is lost, the erotic tingling,

the wool-gabardine mix, its grammatical weave

—you do understand, don't you, by looking?—

never never destined to lose its elasticity,

it was this night I believe but possibly the next

I saw clearly the impossibility of staying

filled with the sensation of being suddenly completed,

also of unknown origin, not shade-giving, not chronological

since the normal growth of boughs is radiating

a system of spoke-wise clubs of green—sleeve-pieces—

never never destined to lose its elasticity

my name being called out now but back, behind,

hissing how many coats do you think it will take

"or try with eyesight to divide" (there is no quarrel)

behind everything the sound of something dripping

a system of spoke-wise clubs of green—sleeve-pieces—

filled with the sensation of suddenly being completed

the wool gabardine mix, the grammatical weave,

the never-never-to-lose-its-elasticity: my name

flapping in the wind like the first note of my absence

hissing how many coats do you think it will take

are you a test case is it an emergency

flapping in the wind the first note of something

overheard nearby an impermanence of structure

watching the lip-reading, there is no quarrel,

I will vanish, others will come here, what is that,

never never to lose the sensation of suddenly being

completed in the wind—the first note of our quarrel—

it was this night I believe or possibly the next

filled with the sensation of being suddenly completed,

I will vanish, others will come here, what is that now

floating in the air before us with stars a test case

that I saw clearly the impossibility of staying

RECOVERED FROM THE STORM

I went out afterwards to see.

Wide silvery hypotheses of memorizing waters.

In them—so deeply—the incomplete pictures.

Twigs, seeds, nuts, limbs scattered over the streets,

distemper's trophies gathering round our footfalls.

I looked at them carefully, wide awake in that monologue.

Some branches thrown down in the middle of things.

Cars not yet venturing. Dusk so blue in its black.

And whole bushes torn from some too-thin origin.

And drowned heads of things strewn wildly through

our singular, tender, green

      clarifications . . .

Am I supposed to put them back together—

these limbs, their leaves, the tiny suctioned twig-end joints—?

these branches shoved deep into my silky glance—?

these maples' outtakes streaked over the lawn—their thorns, their blithe

footnotes . . . ? And the trellis cracked from the weight of the freefall?

And the boxelder standing like an overburdened juggler—

so laden now he cannot remember

the sugary spinnings, the bright fingerings of . . .

Oh limpid puddles with your ditties of fate . . .

There's a shovel by the window.

There's contagion by the gutter.

There's a cartoon upstairs where the children are hidden.

So this is the wingbeat of the underneathly, ticking—

this iridescent brokenness, this wet stunted nothingness—

busy with its hollows—browsing abstractly with its catastrophic wingtips

the tops of our world, ripping pleatings of molecule,

unjoining the slantings, the slippery wrinklings we don't even grasp

    the icily free *made-nature* of yet?

Why are we here in this silly moonlight?

What is the mind meant to tender among splinters?

What was it, exactly, was meant to be *shored?*

Whose dolled-up sorceries *against confusion* now?

The children are upstairs, we will keep them tucked in—

as long as we can, as long as you'll let us.

I hear your pitch. How containment is coughing,

under the leafbits, against the asphalt.

How the new piles of kindling are mossily giggling

    their kerosene cadenza

all long the block in the riddled updrafts.

I pick up and drag one large limb from the path.

OF THE EVER-CHANGING AGITATION IN THE AIR

The man held his hands to his heart as he danced.

He slacked and swirled.

The doorways of the little city

blurred. Something

leaked out,

kindling the doorframes up,

making each entranceway

less true.

And darkness gathered

although it does not fall. . . . And the little dance,

swinging this human all down the alleyway,

nervous little theme pushing itself along,

braiding, rehearsing,

constantly incomplete so turning and tacking—

oh what is there to finish?—his robes made rustic by the reddish swirl,

which grows darker towards the end of the avenue of course,

one hand on his chest,

one flung out to the side as he dances, taps, sings,

on his scuttling toes, now humming a little,

now closing his eyes as he twirls, growing smaller,

why does the sun rise? remember me always dear for I will

return—

liberty spooring in the evening air,

into which the lilacs open, the skirts uplift,

liberty and the blood-eye careening gently over the giant earth,

and the cat in the doorway who does not mistake the world,

eyeing the spots where the birds must eventually land—

from

SWARM

from THE REFORMATION JOURNAL

The wisdom I have heretofore trusted was cowardice, the leaper.

*

I am not lying. There is no lying in me,

*

I surrender myself like the sinking ship,

*

a burning wreck from which the depths will get theirs when the heights have gotten theirs.

*

My throat is an open grave. I hide my face.

*

I have reduced all to lower case.

I have crossed out passages.

I have severely trimmed and cleared.

*

Locations are omitted.

Uncertain readings are inserted silently.

Abbreviations silently expanded.

*

A "he" referring to God may be capitalized
or not.

*

(is crying now)   show me

*

is crying now   (what's wrong)

*

in a strange tree   of atoms   of

*

too few   *more*   no wonder

*

Give me the glassy ripeness

*

Give me the glassy ripeness in failure

*

Give me the atom laying its question at the bottom of nature

*

Send word   Clear fields

*

Make formal event   Walk

*

Turn back

*

Reduce all to lower case   Have reduced all

*

Cross out passages   Have inserted silently

*

is there a name for?

*

glassy ripeness

*

in failure

*

born and raised

*

and you?

*

(go back)   (need more)

*

having lived it   leaves it possible

*

fear   lamentation   shame   ruin   believe me

*

explain   given to

*

explain   born of

*

Absence is odious   to God

*

I'm asking

*

Unseen unseen   the treasure unperceived

*

Unless you compare   the treasure may be lost

*

Oh my beloved   I'm asking

*

More atoms, more days, the noise of the sparrows, of the universals

*

Yet colder here now than in

*

the atom still there at the bottom of nature

*

that we be founded on infinite smallness

*

"which occasions incorruption or immortality"

*

(incorruption because already as little as it can be)

*

(escape square, wasted square, safety square, hopeless square)

"to all except anguish the mind soon adjusts"

*

have reduced, have trimmed, have cleared, have omitted

*

have   abbreviations   silently   expanded

*

to what   avail

*

explain   asks to be followed

explain   remains to be seen

THE VEIL

Exile   Angle of vision.

So steep   the representation.

Desperate   Polite.

A fourth wall   A sixth act.

Centuries lean up into its weave, shudder, go out.

Tongue caresses its entireties.

Look closely for the adjusting of wings,

the knife removed from breast, the noose from

neck,

the acid slippers of eternity being tried on each new foot,

and the patience of understudies, the curtain that cannot rise or fall

over the depth of field. Oh love.

What war did we hope for?

What sleep?

Couldn't the orchestral die down a while—

burning bushes, moving vans—little plazas—eyes of the lion?

What if the rear-view were to open up?

The whole unseeable back where the blood flows off,

drying so quickly,

us broom in hand trying to sweep the front porch off,

every now and then looking up to see how soon.

How soon?

The clouds haul off across.

We tidy up. (*I see*)

War then tidying-up then war. (*I see*)

Shovel the rubble to the roadside. (*gesturing*)

Let the carts loaded with interpreters
                              get by.

It is years.   Goodnight says

the heaven at our backs. (*points*)

Greatness   is sleepy.

Oh my stringed-thing, throat,

when was it I first took this pencil and wrote out

this emptiness you hold now to your ear—

listen: the other place is in it still.

The drawers are full.

Nothing scares off.

I knock on the front

whispering open up, forgive us,

can you grow any more silent?

The windows glint to me

re the straight paths of the right hand,

the refusal that anything be measured
                            or judged,

up here in the shiny
        democracy,

the so-called cup of bitterness,

the so-called train

picking up speed, the so-called

sublime it flatly aims for—

Are we alone? I can never think of you
                    without smiling.

UNDERNEATH (SIBYLLINE)

As if we could tell

if we'd been abandoned.

The battle took so long that soon between the enemies
                                        the bonds
emerged.

Also slowly extinguishing: the sounds of birds, the barking
                                              of dogs.

Planets howl.

Musics rise and fall below the battle sounds.

And you, one being with two parts:

there exists only one instant in which

you can both gain and lose your life.

Remain seated says the voice-over.

(Shouldn't the red light blink?)

Corridor   Curiosity

Appointment   Time

Gods defeated or perhaps   in fact—

(*I can smell it, can't you?*)—

What would you like, someone asked long ago.

Ancient, I'm ancient the one in line before me screams.

I haven't given up on you darling, the hum replies.

I'm planting a wildfire

in your head,

I'm watching I'm remembering,

even though you're dead, you know, you're old tricks—

and this office is swarming with talent.

But what would you *like*?

To stay in your skin?

You've got all of us turning inside-out for you,

but what is it you're suffering from?—

blinking on and off

in the margin,

the free race,

where I goes without saying,

where it begs the question?

Oh bend.

Open your hiding places.

Burn all the letters.

Look in the ashes with both hands.

Finger in there for any bits intact.

                  Wrist-deep

in the fine grains, so cold,

feel further round for fragments,

for any last unburnt

piece of

the crashing of mind,

or any promises (so parched) come down through the sentences
                                    to breathe,

pushing the few bits back to the tiny fire,
            the struck match,

and worrying, and keeping each fragment lit to the very end

by turning it

to every side   every last side—

Look you have to lift the match to it again

because this syllable   is still intact.

from THE REFORMATION JOURNAL (2)

It was during one of these times that
I felt the midst of its suffering,

the presence of its suffering,
like a smile on a beloved face though not exactly

No one   no messenger sent   no image either

One is left to live purely by analogy

By an extreme effort of concentration

Looking just ahead to what appears to be
a pile of wretched flesh in a corner mildly brown

A bit further up the factory   the enormous debt

The sunlight very still on everything animate and in-
                                        animate
making a sound like *it is enough that you exist*

Is it not?

Is not the desire now to lose all personal will?

Come evil, my first person is hidden.

Look, I can rip it off (the pile in the
                corner)

(once it beheld wondrous things)

(that is to say the things that are underneath)

And the narration

which relates the things

(but they must   be true)

The path of thought also now too bright

So that its edges cut

So that I'm writing this in the cold

keeping the parts from finding the whole again

page after page, unstitched, speaking for sand

Look I push the book off my desk

into the flood

"Let him be prepared to give the poison twice or
even thrice if necessary"

As when feeling you watch my sleeping body

PRAYER

(after Hölderlin)

Should we not speak of you?
Should you ring in us   as an idle caprice

pressed into   service,
should we not, you deed rampaging destiny, furious,

pressing voice into service,
as if the hurling of hot arrows,

pressing the good into your service,
making it play for you?

And yet you will veil our eyes
that we not perish.

Hard burden. Names and names.
Likewise the river.

I called you once and thought you once.
You travel down to me on your allotted paths,

a light embrace, miraculously omnipresent.

UNDERNEATH (CALYPSO)

1

Sing to me   of time and time again

being driven   off course

to face   another audience

bewitching   craving to hold

him   back

I apologize   to coincidence

I apologize   to necessity

Let happiness try to receive the dead

Apologize   to the war I steal him from

You must forgive   this veil

It's like a laughing   time and again

I wanted to be   everything

I know nothing can justify   the veil

Be brave   Let it descend

2

Why should the exile   return home?

Era?   Period?

Discover: Calypso has shuffled the deck.

Has veiled the early with the late.

Has veiled sequence.

Remembering violent   as it must be,

and it all now middle-time.   Sleep, love.

What must be   inferred under

the blemished   mantling   shimmers.

How else to keep you.

I apologize to history.

I covered the story with all these words.

Overgrown with eyes.

3

The stress and drag of looking.   Look.

Shuffled the deck   to veil phenomena, yes.

Strike me says each thing.

Resurrect me   in *my*   flesh.

Do not pass through me.

4

Look how our mouths   are bared.

And those, still strapped in their seats, the others.

I am held to myself   by force.

No voyage   home

over blossoming's   broad back.

Forced down instead   into the stalk.

Let your soul slip through   radiance

Let not radiance cling to you   Push through

5

How we walk the aisle: in flames.

Frothing time back   into its corner.

In anguish here   under the veil.

Going broken   before some altar.

UNDERNEATH (13)

needed   explanation

because of the mystic nature   of the theory

and our reliance   on collective belief

I could not visualize the end

the tools that paved the way broke

the body the foundation the exact copy of the real

our surfaces were covered

our surfaces are all covered

actual hands appear but then there is writing

in the cave   we were deeply impressed

as in addicted to results

oh and dedication training   the idea of loss of life

in our work we call this emotion

how a poem enters into the world

there is nothing wrong with the instrument

as here I would raise my voice but

the human being and the world cannot be equated

aside from the question of whether or not we are alone

and other approaches to nothingness

(the term "subject")(the term "only")

also *opinion* and *annihilation*

(the body's minutest sensation of time)

(the world, it is true, has not yet been destroyed)

intensification   void

we are amazed

uselessness is the last form love takes

so liquid till the forgone conclusion

here we are, the forgone conclusion

so many messages transmitted they will never acquire meaning

do you remember   my love my archive

touch me (here)

give birth to   a single idea

touch where it does not lead to war

show me   exact spot

climb the stairs

lie on the bed

have faith

nerves wearing only moonlight lie down

lie still patrol yr cage

be a phenomenon

at the bottom below the word

intention, lick past it

rip   years

find the burning matter

love allows it (I think)

push past the freedom (smoke)

push past   intelligence (smoke)

whelm   sprawl

(favorite city)   (god's tiny voices)

hand over mouth

let light arrive

let the past strike us and go

drift   undo

if it please the dawn

lean down

say   hurt   undo

in your mouth be pleased

where does it say

where does it say

this is the mother tongue

there is in my mouth a ladder

climb down

presence of world

impassable   gap

pass

I am beside myself

you are inside me   as history

We exist   Meet me

from

NEVER

PRAYER

Over a dock railing, I watch the minnows, thousands, swirl
themselves, each a minuscule muscle, but also, without the
way to *create* current, making of their unison (turning, re-
                                    infolding,
entering and exiting their own unison in unison) making of themselves a
visual current, one that cannot freight or sway by
minutest fractions the water's downdrafts and upswirls, the
dockside cycles of finally-arriving boat-wakes, there where
they hit deeper resistance, water that seems to burst into
itself (it has those layers), a real current though mostly
invisible sending into the visible (minnows) arrowing
                        motion that forces change—
this is freedom. This is the force of faith. Nobody gets
what they want. Never again are you the same. The longing
is to be pure. What you get is to be changed. More and more by
each glistening minute, through which infinity threads itself,
also oblivion, of course, the aftershocks of something
at sea. Here, hands full of sand, letting it sift through
in the wind, I look in and say take this, this is
what I have saved, take this, hurry. And if I listen
now? Listen, I was not saying anything. It was only
something I did. I could not choose words. I am free to go.
I cannot of course come back. Not to this. Never.
It is a ghost posed on my lips. Here: never.

IN / SILENCE

I try to hold my lie in mind.
My thinking one thing while feeling another.
My being forced. Because the truth
is a thing one is not permitted to *say*.
That it is reserved for silence,
a buttress in silence's flyings, its motions
always away from source; that it is re-
served for *going* too, for a deeply
artifactual spidery form, and how it can, gleaming,
yet looking still like mere open air, mere light,
catch in its syntax the necessary sacrifice.
Oh whatever that might be. How for song
I looked today long and hard at a singing bird,
small as my hand, inches from me, seeming
to puff out and hold something within, something that

                                  makes

wind ruffle his exterior more—watched
him lift and twist a beak sunlight made burnt-silver
as he tossed it back—not so much to let
anything *out* but more to carve and then to place firmly in the

                               listening space
                               around him

a piece of inwardness: no visible
passaging-through: no inner complication and release:
no passage from an inner place—a mechanism
of strings, bone, hollow
chamber—no native immaterial quiver time turns material—

then towards [by mechanisms ancient and invisible] expression,

and the tragic of all upward motion—

then it all lost in the going aloft with the as yet

                          unsung—then

the betrayal (into the clear morning air)

of the source of happiness into mere (sung) happiness.

Although there is between the two, just at the break

of silentness, a hovering, almost a penitent

                        hesitation, an

intake, naked, before any dazzling release

of the unfree into the seeming free, and it seems

it goes elsewhere, and the near (the engine) overruns

into the truly free. This till the last stars be counted?

This plus the mind's insistent coming back and coming back?

This up against that coming back. The death of

uncertainty. The song that falls upon the listener's *eye*,

that seeks the sleek minimum of the meaningless *made*.

Here in the morning light. In matter's massive/muscular/venerable holding-in

of all this flow. Next door the roses flow.

Blood in the hand that reaches for them flows.

DUSK SHORE PRAYER

The creeping revelation of shoreline.
The under-shadowed paisleys scripting wave-edge down-
                                   slope
on the barest inclination, sun making of each
                mile-long wave-retreat
a golden translucent forward downgoing,
golden sentences writ on clearest moving waters,
moving their meaninglessness on (not *in*) the moving of the
                                waters
(which feels tugged)(the rows of scripting
[even though it's a trick] adamant with
self-unfolding)(wanting the eye to catch and take
dominant final-hold, feel the thickest rope of
                waterlipped
                scripting
to be a producing of a thing that speaks [to whom
one does not know, but a true speech])—to believe this truly,
                        not in metaphor—
to put it in the blank in which one *sees*,
and then into the blank in which one *is*,
to separate *I am* from *I have being* from *I am
apart*. And not to want to *be*. And never to be
emptied by the wound of meaning.
The gash of likeness. The stump interpretation.
Spelled from the living world. Grown sharper by
this sighting. As sun goes down. Until it glimmers in
the tiny darkness and the human will comes to the end.
Having it go before one's looking goes. The summer
at one's back. The path back barely findable.

GULLS

Those neck-pointing out full bodylength and calling
outwards over the breaking waves.
Those standing in waves and letting them come and
                        go over them.
Those gathering head-down and over some one
                      thing.
Those still out there where motion is
primarily a pulsing from underneath
and the forward-motion so slight they lay
their stillness on its swelling and falling
and let themselves swell, fall . . .
Sometimes the whole flock rising and running just
as the last film of darkness rises
leaving behind, also rising and falling in
               tiny upliftings,
almost a mile of white underfeathers, up-turned, white spines
                     gliding over the wet
sand, in gusts, being blown down towards
          the unified inrolling awayness
          of white. All things turning white through
breaking. The long red pointing of lowering sun
going down on (but also streaking in towards) whoever
might be standing at the point-of-view place
from which this watching. This watching being risen
from: as glance: along the red
blurring and swaying water-path:
to the singular redness: the glance a

being-everywhere-risen-from: everywhere
cawing, mewing, cries where a
single bird lifts heavily
just at shoreline, rip where
its wing-tips (both) lap
backwash, feet still in
the wave-drag of it, to coast
on top of its own shadow and then down to not
landing.

*

Also just under the wave a thickening where
sun breaks into two red circles upon the
                    carried frothing—
white and roiling, yes, yet unbreakably red—red pushed (slicked) under
                    each wave (tucked) and, although breaking, always
                    one—(as if from the back-end-of-distance red)—
and that *one* flowing to here to
slap the red it carries in glisten-sheets
up onto shore and (also as if *onto*)
my feet.

*

[Or onto my feet, then into my eyes] where red turns into "sun" again.
So then it's sun in surf-breaking water: incircling, smearing: mind not
knowing if it's still "wave," breaking on
itself, small glider, or if it's "amidst" (red turning feathery)
or rather "over" (the laciness of foambreak) or just *what*—(among
the line of also smearingly reddening terns floating out now
on the feathery backedge of foambroken
looking)—*it is*.

*

The wind swallows my words one
                              by
one. The words leaping too, over their own
                                    staying.
Oceanward too, as if being taken
                        away
into splash—my clutch of
                words
swaying and stemming from my
                    saying, no
echo. No stopping on the temporarily exposed and drying rock
                                                out there
to rub or rest where nothing else
                        grows.
And truly swift over the sands.
As if most afraid of being re-
                    peated.
Preferring to be dissolved to
                designation,
backglancing stirrings,
wedged-in between unsaying and
                    forgetting—
what an enterprise—spoken out by
                    me as if
to *still* some last place, place becoming even as I speak
                                    unspeakable—
"We shall have early fruit
this year" one of the shades along the way
                            calls out,
and "from the beginning" (yet further on). Words: always face-down:

listening falling upon them (as if from

                above):

flinging itself upon them: them open and attached

                so hard to

                what they carry:

the only evidence in them of having

                been.

And yet how they want to see behind themselves—

                as if there is something

back there, always, behind these rows I

                gnaw the open with—

feeling them rush a bit and crane to see beneath themselves—

twisting on their stems to see behind—as if there were a

                        sun

back there they need, as if it's a betrayal,

this single forward-facing: reference: dream of: ad-

                mission: re

semblance: you are not alone:

slowly in the listener the prisoners emerge:

slowly in you reader they stand like madmen facing into the wind:

nowhere is there any trace of blood

spilled in the service of kings, or love, or for the sake of honor,

or for some other reason.

EBBTIDE

I am a frequency, current flies through. One has

to ride

the spine.

No peace [of mind][of heart], among the other

frequencies. How often and how hard are answerings.

The surf, receding, leaves successive

hem-line trims of barely raised institching sand—

bridal-wreath puckerings—

glassy (this side), packed smooth (that).

Making one's way one sees the changes.

What took place before one

looked.

Snakeskin of darker sands in with the light.

Slightly more raised and wider alligator-skins.

Crabtracks' wild unfocusings around firm holes.

The single tubefish, dead, long as a snake, half-snout,

rolled over and over as the waves pick up, return, return

less often, go away. For a while he is incandescent

white, then blue, deep green, then white again, until he's

left, half-turned,

eyes sandy till one wave, come back

this far as if in error, cleans him off.

Greenish with rising / falling weed-debris, shoremist

fingering long streaks of sun.

Graphed beachlength on the scallop-edged lapping retreat:

christmas-ornament red shrimp

punctually along the highs of each

upskirting arc—prongs upright,

stiff. Swift ticks of sunlight count them

out.

Who has enough? A little distance

back

two vultures feeding on a pelican. Later, claws and beak

float in the brack. Foam-bits lace-up the edge

of the retreat. Something feels like it's not

coming back. In the tidepool

sand-grains advance along a long

walled avenue, in ranks—at the conjunction of

two rocks, algae

signaling the entry point—(swarming but

swaying in

unison, without advancing) (waiting for

some arrival)

(the channel of them quickening)(the large espousal)(light

beginning now to *touch* what had been only

underwater story)—

until the gleaming flow of particles is finally

set down, is

stilled: the grains

drop down and mat, silt in, begin to dry: the wandering tribe is

gone, the

city's gone, the waiting gone. The individual grains

are not discernible. I'm squatting so I hear

sand sucking water in. Gravity. Glistening.

I take a stick and run it through

the corridor of wilderness.

It fills a bit with water the first time. Is self-erased.

The second time it does not fill. It leaves a

mark where

my stick ran. I make

another (cursive) mark. How easily it bends to cursive, snakes towards

thought.

Looking back

I see the birds eating the bird. The other way my

gaze can barely reach shore-break.

The (little) weight of the stick in my hand. The meditation

place demands. My frequency. This hand, this

sugar-stalk. The cane-fields in the back of us,

the length of tubefish back there too. And

if I write my name. And how mist rounds the headland

till the sea

is gone. One feels word should be sent us

from some source. It is all

roar and cry and suck and snap. The pebbles on the

pebbles roll. One feels one has in custody

what one cannot care for for long. Too much is

asked. Nothing is coming back the way it was.

But one can wait for the next hem, next bride,

next oscillation, comedy. Done, the birds fly

off. I can see through the trees,

through the cane grove, palm grove, out far enough into

the clearing where

the spine of the picked-clean story shines.

EVOLUTION

How old are you?

As old as until now.

Under the kelp-bed razorclams turning to find

                                                  purchase.

Young things shooting first-times and retaining

                                                 precedence.

Razors digging backwards and down,

spurting spittle-bits of sea

to equalize descent.

Do you believe that after you die some part of you

                                                  lives on?

Do you pray in hope of reward?

Do you agree or disagree with the following

                                                statement:

it bothers me my life did not turn out as I

                                                expected.

Also there are people on the beach.

And wind accepted by waterfilm.

Look: acceptance has a shape.

And fate—is it accepted by waterfilm?

And how we must promise things.

Do you pray in hope of reward.

Do you pray without hope of reward.

What is it has been gone a long time?

How long is the slightest chance?

Everything in sunlight

improvising backwards,

scratching phrases in a rapid jitter,

where the mind above it begins, ends, tries to get up

and move

towards or away from.

You'll feel the so-called music strut hard against

the downsuck.

Also someone's shadow going to purchase a beverage.

Also everything in sunlight trying to become bodied by something

else,

the whole retreating ocean laying

microscopic and also slightly larger fiercely-lit

kelp in streaks of action—

long sentences with branchlike off-widths indicating

acceleration brought forth

and left-off, phrases of gigantic backing-off

from a previously

held shore,

rivulets of sand left visible in raised inscription

whitening where moistened—questionlike—algebraic—

regarding the long leave-taking—

We are ourselves walking to the right.

The noon hour is itself always a firstness

of something.

Also, elsewhere, who is hungry?

How small are they? How? I step on parts of

faces, only parts. A whole face, what is that? From here

it seems hard to make out, also a very empty

thing. Like the border of a nationstate.

Being comes into this, idles,

over the interminable logic of

manyness, the demand that *something exist.*

Bending to look close, a

spiking-up and forth of burrowings,

channelings, a turning, a re-turning on

itself where the broad

nouns of large clamshells

flayed open by gulls lie

in punctuating sunlit stillness

on top of a thing which but for

their stillness and expulsion

has no top. The seagulls

hurrying, dragging and retrieving. Also

pecking in place and dropping and

lifting. Sometimes stepping backwards in order to

drag and loosen. Also the drag of the slantline

downtilted towards ocean's sucking further still of

streams of water towards

itself. Of course the future

wasn't there before at all.

This all first time and then again first

                time.

I feel reproach. Eyes closed I touch my face.

My hand hovers like the very question of my face

              over my face.

G says, breathing beside me, that firstness is not, in any case,

a characteristic of experience.

He speaks of the long chain back

to the beginning of "the world" (as he calls it) and then, at last,

              to the great *no*

beginning. I feel the *no* begin.

Subsequence hums tinily all round me,

erasing my tracks. Oh bright/morning. This

            morning.

Look: what looks like retreating is not exactly so.

Sunlight makes of exactness an issue.

No issuing *forth* of matter

because of sunlight. But sun's

up-sucking also at work. And how

it seems to have weight,

pushing the originally pillowy kelp-beds

down, flattening them where they

give up water, unthickening their

pastures as the tunneling-away from

that gigantic drying drives

the almost-imperceptible downwards:

first glitter then more unchangeable shine slowly being

forced into the vast top of the

beachwide beds. Drying out and

hardening, the beds force light

                  back.

Back across what resides inside.

White closed-in part of gazing-out.

Bothered by the ease of touch.

As if one should open out and spill, again.

Sound in the sun now muted

(is there an inherent good)

as the ruffling back-roar recedes

(is there inherent good in people)—

Sound becoming particular and pricked

with syncopations of singularities—

peeps, insucks, snaps—where light is

                  in domain.

What good is my silence for, what would it hold

                  inside, keeping it free?

Sing says the folding water on stiller water—

one running through where the other's breaking. Sing me

something (the sound of the low wave-breaking)

(the tuning-down where it deposits life-matter on

the uphill of shore)(also the multiplicity

of deepenings and coverings where whiteness rises as a

                  manyness)

(as the wave breaks over its own breaking)

(to rip in unison)(onto its backslide)—

of something sing, and singing, disagree.

from

OVERLORD

OTHER

For a long time I used to love the word *now*. I murmured its

tiniest of songs to myself as a child when alone. *Now now now*

now I sang, not much knowing where we were. Until, before I knew it,

it put forth its liquid melody, and time, shimmering, began to flow

nearly inaudible, alongside the crickets if it was summer, alongside the penumbral

clock if it was the kitchen, alongside the tapping of the wintered lilac's branches on the

violet-shadowed

walls that held the garden,

if it was wind. Where were we, in fact? *Now now* the adults used to say

meaning pay attention, meaning the thing at hand, the crucial thing, has these

slippery sides: this *now* its one slope, this *now* its

other. The thing itself, the essential thing, is in between. Don't blink. Don't

miss it. Pay attention. It's a bullet.

All those years, before I became lost, I lived a different life.

One where you can go back. I thought each new

now, new

note, plucked from the as-yet-unpronounced, covered up a footstep

of the retreating God.

Where was it just before, I wondered, as it moved away in concentric circles

from the place the finger had triggered. *Tap tap* drummed my mother's hand

without her knowing on the kitchen table

in the dim end of afternoon. To keep away waiting. There is no

waiting. There will never be tomorrow. Nonetheless you do suddenly fall asleep, and then,

there it is again, when just as suddenly your eyes open, it floods in, and you

are full, and the song begins. One day

I woke up, I was

sick, in bed, my first time, since beginning, since beginning school, since the becoming of my self.

I looked for the notes but walls slid in. A weight

descended. I was waiting. The first time. What age could I have been?

The house gave forth its ticking and tapping. One-time sounds occurred—a shutter

                                            snapped,

a heavy clink where keys were dropped, the sweet dry

clack where a pinecone hits

gravel below. A mourning dove. Once. Then after a while, again, once.

What else could be inside me? That's when I heard

what makes me break this silence and speak to you this way.

I heard my name, as always, called out into the classroom as the schoolday began.

PEPPER, Jorie. I sat up. I knew what space it floated into, everyone waiting.

I heard it said the second time into the grayish morninglight

over the rows and rows of chairs, the gleaming fullness of them, empty, as children stood.

There was nothing I could do. I saw it as I heard it—"absent"—

said out into the room. Heard the silence that followed it.

Sitting up, I looked about. The tree beyond the windowpane flowed out to its bark.

It ticked out its being to its leaftips, down into its roots. *It could not be*

                                absent. The blue

cup on the dresser, its tiny blue stream, crabapples in bloom, one bird sitting on

the handrail of the bridge—what of it could ever retreat,

leaving only part of itself present?—or the clouds—on cup, in sky—or the tasseled

                                        fringe of

curtain, door, wicker chair with rose-pattern pillow, saffron lampshade with cream-

brocaded border. . . . I don't know if I cried out,

but they came running up to see what was wrong.

This is what is wrong: we, only we, the humans, can retreat from ourselves and

                                      not be

                                    altogether here.

We can be part full, only part, and not die. We can be in and out of here, now,

at once, and not die. The little song, the little river, has banks. We can pull up

                          and sit on the banks. We can pull back

from the being of our bodies, we can live in a

portion of them, we can be absent, no one can tell.

DAWN DAY ONE

(Dec 21, 2003)

A gunshot. The second, but the first I heard.

Then the walls of the room, streaked with first light, shot

                                        into place.

Then, only then, did my eyes open.

We come about first, into waking, as an *us*, I

think. Sometime between the first and second instant

there is still the current that carries one in

and deposits one in singleness. The body's weight is

a beaching. Back behind, or underneath: infinity

or something which has no consequence. Then consequence, which

feels like walls and the uprighting of self one has to do

in them, then the step one has to take once roused, and how it

puts one back on the walking-path one stepped off of

last night. Zeno reasoned we would

never get there. Reason in fact never gets there.

But we step back onto the path each time.

How long have you been yours, are you tired, are you

in a hurry, are you sitting down, is that stillness

still your pathway which you enter

                    now only with

your mind—which keeps on stepping mind you—

until it doesn't and the stopping

                happens again.

Are your eyes shut? I put cream on my lids

and rub it in. I feel my eyes in there under the skin.

How impersonal are they, these hardnesses, barely

attached, in their loosely protected sacks.

Tony tells me how, in the lab, they cast an image

—a cross in this case—onto the gaze of a monkey then

"sacrifice

the monkey" and how, when examined, the neurons in the

visual cortex

actually form the imprint of

the cross. It would have been, the cross (except under very

unusual circumstances), erased

by the next image. Hence the need for

sacrifice. Of what is it made, I ask. Of cells, of *active*

cells, he says. Is it imprinted, I ask. No. It

would have disappeared and been replaced except

the creature was stilled. I like it they

use the word *stilled*. Then the back

of the cave in there with its cross of cells. Which will

dissolve as the "next instant". Some arguments

continue this way ad infinitum. And

infinitum *is* one path, but you can't

really get onto its promenade, its boardwalk, by

speculation. "Therefore" is another way to walk,

therefore the fast Achilles can never best the slow

tortoise. Zeno inferred yet another way.

And yes, now space and time can be subdivided

infinitely many times. But isn't this sad?

By now hasn't a sadness crept in?

I put my hands over both my eyes and lie

still. I think. The paradox says that you can never leave

the room in which you are right now. First walk

half the distance to the door, then half again, and so on. These eyes,

under my hands, I looked at in the mirror yesterday.

Everything of course was silver, my skin, my gaze,

and then the eyes, held in

        their lids.

Looked hard into that room.

Looked everywhere, all the way to the back. The

                  back

                  tells me

I have to come back here, here to the front, there is

no further I can go. One takes smaller and smaller steps

according to Zeno to try to leave the room. If you return now

to the glass, you can look *at* your eyes. After a short

time, very short if you hold fast, don't blink, just stare,

you will be looking at *an other*. A silver one. I promise

you, go do it now, you will see it, it is not you.

It is more exactly not-you than anyone you've

ever seen. Keep staring. Even Achilles must take

smaller and smaller steps. Even so he can never win.

Before Zeno there was Pythagoras. Before Pythagoras humans

did not understand—that is the verb that is used—that results

had to be proved. That there is an edifice

you can build, level upon level, from first principles,

using axioms, using logic. Finally you have a house

which houses you. Now look at you.

Are you an entire system of logic and truth?

Are you a pathway with no body ever really on it?

Are you shatterable if you took your fist now to

this face that looks at you as you hold to your stare?

Here. You are at the beginning of something. At the exact

beginning. Ok. This is awakening

number two in here, in this poem. Then there are

these: me: you: you *there*. I'm actually staring up at

you, you know, right here, right from the pool of this page.

Don't worry where else I am, I am here. Don't

worry if I'm still alive, you are.

UPON EMERGENCE

Have I that to which to devote my
self? Have I devotion? The shoes, the
clothes? The drowning of appetites, as the chariots
were drowned? I sit at the very edge
of the garden, paying out my attention.
The moving and moving of the mottled interminable
forms—the deepness in the unseen, the
different deepnesses in the lisping way the gaze
takes time to alight. Nothing is solid as itself—
that too. A style to the visible world which is—yes like
death—but also like a spume, or the way music seems to formulate
words—a style which I can feel slip free of
point of view and gaze, the artificer mind
making explicit what is not—as in the version of a place
                                        inside a place. Is it a
future that I see? Right here, just underneath this rock I
lift—brood of tiny helmets going everywhere towards defeat—is it
sunlight laying itself hard
on the geranium leaves—which it also
fattens—an existent thing, the sun, yes, and yet, if so, *where*
does it exist? The fine hairs on the geranium leaves stand up
and catch the light. If you bend close you'll see the
future there—do you remember? "Do you re-
member" is that what devotion says? Do not forget to
remember. I feel, inside, a fantastic pressing of blood against
this skin. I hold my open hands up, here,
before my face, I listen hard to them.
Clouds press. The passings of their shadows press

onto each palm. There is no underneath.

It is all souvenir.

The bird that was just feeding here

is now appearing in my mind. The blood

inside me now must take it round and round. Hardly changed,

it bends and pecks at the last bits of seed below

the lavender. Riding on the blood in me,

its wings spread out. And also bloody, yes, the grass

of mind, bright red its stalks. Also glints on its claws, its

wingtips rising up, above the streams—of me? in me?—

borne round and round by my sticky devotion here, my *thinking* it. . . .

So this is the source of evil? Of course I know

how small it is. But what lies buried at the core

of this holding-in-mind, this final place in which we are

compelled to bury it? We live in time. It is a

holiday. All round it timelessness which will begin again,

yet still, for now, sticks to *one* time like remnant rain

after the place is solidly in place under fresh sun.

Concerning the gods I have no means.

But from this path what is it must be

seen, what must be thought and spoken of—from this,

what is it that is taken from the visible—

what is it that cannot be given back

in *any* form—which burns off—without

residue—just by coming into contact with

the verb of human inwardness? How helpless they are—

both sides—can the gods really know?—the

ineffable pain, amazement, thronging drift

of accident whereby freedom of world, of

subject, are forced to give way? Oh

"path of inquiry"! All of it unable to die

or kill. Also unable to stay calmly under-

neath, or *in* any arrival place—no hell, even,

no hell. . . . I know it is only the visible world.

But nothing is small enough to escape us.

Can I devote myself to setting it free?

Where, where is it free? Before I think it,

what is its state? And if I summon it

to mind, if I begin to summon it? Unbearable

                tyranny. Tiny

monster picking up the reins of my eyes.

The chariots of the sun "says" the tiniest god (definition).

Beyond whispers the hillside, the paragraph

break, the insuck of breath before this

rest. *Where is your brother* hisses the page.

SOLDATENFRIEDHOF

(German Cemetery, La Cambe, Normandy, 2003,
Computer Terminal)

"To find a fallen person," it says, "push green key."

Fill in name, last name, first name, I put in

Klein. 210 Kleins in the Soldatenfriedhof.

I scroll. Klein stays the same.

The first name changes, rank, row, plot.

No. The graveyard changes too. At 88 Klein's in

Colleville (US graveyard). At 93 he's in the British one (Bayeux).

Have you found your fallen person says the program

when I go back to the home page. No slot for

nationality. None for religion. Just date of

                              birth,

then rank, row, plot, and field come forth. I'm staring at

                                      the soundless

screen. Keys very large for easy use.

Back through the doorway there's the

field. 21,222 German soldiers. Some named, some not.

Inside the office now a wide face looking up.

When is the last time a new man was found, I ask.

Here it is full, he says, people now go to Saint André.

So there are no new bodies being found?

Oh no. No, no. Just last month eight—

here look, pulling a red file from a stack.

Look—and it's open—here, you'll see.

A name, a question mark, a print of teeth of which two

(lost after death) marked "lost after death." A plastic

baggie holds an oval metal tag, almost

illegible, now placed into

my hand. The other baggie he snaps open: here:

a button: we mostly tell them from the buttons:

this was a paratrooper: you can see from

the size, the color of the casing. The sleeve

of something other than time, I think,

slides open to reveal, nested, as in a pod, this seed, hard, dark, how does he

make out its

identity—a paratrooper—a German one—each people's

buttons different—if it's a German, we get called—if he is ours

we begin work—whatever clothing still exists—part of

a boot,

a lace, can get you back

the person—a metal clip—the stitching of a kind of

cloth. There were so many kinds of fiber then. Then

as much soil as we can get—bone-fragments when there are—

how fast flesh turns to soil again—that is why clothing is

so good.

Where there are teeth too it is good—

we will be able to notify the family.

There is great peace in knowing your person is found.

Mostly in Spring when the land is plowed.

Sometimes when they widen roads.

Many were put in with the apple trees.

One feels, from the way they are placed, the burying

was filled with kindness. I don't really know why, but it is

so. I turn the oval in my hand. Soil on it still, inside the chiseled number-

group, deeper

in the 3's and 8's, so that it's harder to make out the whole.

The boy is 17 he says.

What if he hadn't been found.

What if he is now found.

What does he re-enter.

Saint André de Champigny will receive

some earth, jaw, teeth, buttons, dog-tag, an

insignia, hair, bones of most of one

right hand. When more than one have been found

together, the official of the graves registration department

—this man with soft large hands holding the folder out—

portions out enough human remains

to make up as many people as possible.

The possible person: a tooth is enough. *Anything*

                                             will do

really, he says looking up, almost inaudibly.

With whom is he pleading.

Behind him now the field where in 1947 American bodies, and parts-of, put here

                                                          temporarily,

were dug up and moved for the final time

to their last resting place, to the American Normandy War Memorial—

and these available German parts and wholes pulled from their

holding grounds and placed in openings Americans

                                        released.

Forgive me says the man still in his seat,

I have been rude, I did not mean (gets up)

my name is _____, here is my card.

May I hold the button a moment longer?

You from under the apple orchard,

you still not found in my field,

and the mole hacking through,

and the rabbits at dawn eating,

and the bird I cannot identify,

you, meaninglessness,

speak out—what do you hate—what do you hate—

SPOKEN FROM THE HEDGEROWS

I was Floyd West (1st Division) I was born in Portia Arkansas Feb 6
1919 We went through Reykjavik Iceland through the North Atlantic through the
                                                          wolf packs
That was 1942 I was Don Whitsitt I flew a B-26 medium bomber
Number 131657 called the Mississippi Mudcat I was a member of

The 387th Bomb Group and then later the 559th Bomb
Squadron. Picked up the Mudcat in Mt. Clemens Michigan
Flew over our whole group four squadrons sixteen planes each
from Hunter Field at Savannah Georgia then to Langley Field at

Norfolk Virginia from there to Grenier Field at Manchester New Hampshire
In each place stayed a day or two
From Grenier went on to port of embarkation
which was Presque Isle, Maine, then started across, first to Goose Bay, Labrador,

then to Bluie West One, Greenland, then over the cap to
Mick's Field, Iceland. Made landfall at Stornoway, Scotland, from there
down to Prestwick, north London, finally Station 162 at Chipping
Ongar. My name was Dan, 392nd Squadron of the 367th Fighter Group

March 21 boarded the *Duchess of Bedford* in NY,
an old English freighter which had been converted
to bring over the load of German prisoners, whom we replaced

going back to England. Slept below decks in hammocks.
April 3rd arrived at Scotland, and, following a beautiful trip through
the country, arrived at Stoney Cross, ten miles from the Channel—

it was a beautiful moonlit night. I was known as Bob. I was in
D Company. My number was 20364227. I was born Feb 3,
1925, Bristol, Tennessee. We embarked on the HMS

Queen Mary, stripped, painted dull gray, hammocks installed with
troops sleeping in shifts. The *Queen* was capable of making twenty-eight knots
and therefore traveled unescorted, since it could outrun any

sub. Walter, given name, 29th Division. We crossed on the *Queen Mary.* The
swimming pool was covered over, that's where most of us slept.
My name was Alan, Alan Anderson, 467th Anti-Aircraft Artillery. I was given

birth November 1, 1917, Winchester, Wisconsin. They took us to
Fort Dix for England. We took the northern route in the extreme rough sea of
January. It was thought that this would confuse the

German subs. It didn't exactly work that way.
A convoy ahead of us by a few days was hit, many ships sank.
I saw the bodies of so many sailors and soldiers floating by us

with all the other debris and ice on the water. The name given me
was John, born September 13, '24, in Chattanooga, but raised
in Jacksonville. I was a person, graduated high school in '42,

crossed over on the *Ile de France,* a five-decker, ten thousand on board.
They loaded over twenty on the *Queen Mary*
there on the other side of the pier. My name was Ralph, Second Class Pharmacist's Mate,
July 4 received orders to Norfolk. There's no describing

crossing the Atlantic in winter. We couldn't stay in our bunks
without being strapped in and fastened to metal pipes on
each side. We had one meal a day. My name, Robert, was put to me

in Atchison, Kansas, United States, August 15, 1916, year of the

Lord we used to figure on, there, in the 149th Engineer Combat Battalion,

which arrived Liverpool, England, January 8 1944. It rained every day.

From there we were taken to the town of Paignton. The authorities

would go down the road, and the truck would stop, and they'd say

"All right, three of you out here" and they'd march you to a house and say to
the owner,

"all right, these are your Americans. They are going to be staying with you."

LITTLE EXERCISE

The screen is full of voices, all of them holding their tongues.

Certain things have to be "undergone," yes.

To come to a greater state of consciousness, yes.

Let the face show itself through the screen.

Let the organizing eyes show themselves.

Let them float to the surface of this shine and glow there.

The world now being killed by its children. Also its guests.

An oracle?—a sniper, a child beater, a dying parent in the house,

a soil so overfed it cannot hold a root system in place?

Look—the slightest wind undoes the young crop.

Are we "beyond salvation"? Will you not speak?

Such a large absence—shall it not compel the largest presence?

Can we not break the wall?

And can it please *not be a mirror* lord?

PRAYING (*Attempt of May 9 '03*)

I don't know where to start. I don't think my face

in my hands is right. Please don't let us destroy

Your world. No *the* world. I know I know nothing. I know I

can't use you like this. It feels better if I'm on

my knees, if my eyes are pressed shut so I can see

the other things, the tiniest ones. Which can still escape

us. Am I human. Please show me mercy. No please show

a way. If I look up all the possibility that you

might be there goes away. I need to be curled up this

way, face pressed, knees pulled up tight. I know

there are other ways, less protected, more expressive of

surrender. But here I can feel the whole crushing

emptiness on my back. Especially on my shoulders.

I thought just now how that emptiness could be my wings.

That you were there, maybe, laughing. That the room above me,

here, before dawn, its two windows black, this

pillow pressed down hard against me, how it, how all of it,

made up the wings. There is a reason I

have to go fast. Have to try to slide into

something I can feel the beginning of. Right

here in my pushed-down face. Right

where eyes are pressed

so sleep doesn't go there anymore.

And the mirror—well that is another way if you wish. If you

look in for a very long time. But here, I did this other thing

again. (Here)(I write the open parenthesis, press my face,

try again, then lift, close)(then this clause to explain)
(to whom?)(always wanting to be forgiven)(not seen)(no)—See,
it is already being lost here, the channel is filling
in, these words—ah—these, these—
how I don't want *them* to be the problem too, there are
so many other obstacles, can't these be just a part of
my body, look (put my head down again)(am
working in total dark)(maybe this will not be
legible)—my ears covered to go further—maybe
if I had begun otherwise, maybe if I had
been taught to believe in You, I needed evidence,
others seem not to need it, they do not seem to me
graced, but yesterday when I asked Don he said yes, he
                              was sure, yes,
everything was His plan, so it is a lapse of faith
to worry, you will have noted I cannot say "Your
plan," and now, as if dawn were creeping in, the
feeling of the reader is coming in, the one towards which
this tilts, like the plant I watched a long time yesterday the
head of, and then the stem itself,
to see if it turned towards the light as the light arrived,
I would say it did, very slightly, and I
                    could not *see it,*
though I never lifted my gaze, and tried very hard to blink only
when physically impossible not to, and yes, yes, in the end it
was in a different direction, I had marked where we started
so I knew for sure, although of course I know nothing, I could
begin this story anywhere, maybe I will open my
eyes now, although I have gotten nowhere and will
                              find myself
still just here, in the middle of my exactly given years, on
my knees naked in my room before dawn, the pillow

wet of course but what of it, nothing nothing comes of it,

                      out there where the

garbage truck will begin any second now, where I

can feel the whitening reefs (which

I have only read about)(if that means anything)(yes/no) under there where

                              they are,

the waters filtering through them, the pH wrong, the

terrible bleaching occurring, the temperature, what

is a few degrees, how fine are we supposed

to be, I am your instrument if you would only use me, a

degree a fraction of a degree in the beautiful thin

water, flowing through, finding as it is meant to *every*

hollow, and going in, carrying its devastation in, but looking so

simple, and a blue I have never seen, with light still in its

body as light is in mine here I believe, yes,

light a chemical analysis would reveal,

something partaking of the same photons

in this pillow, this paint on the wall, this wall,

which if I open my eyes will be five inches from my face,

which (the coral reefs having caverns) I try to go into—

because I can make myself very small is that a gift from you,

I think it might be one of the great gifts, that I can *make*

myself very small and go in, in from this room, down into the

fibrous crenellations of the reef, which if you look close are formed

by one node clipping onto another, and then

the rounding-up as the damage occurs, as the weight is lost, now the coral

                            in with the

trucks, pipeknock kicking in, it is beginning

again—oh—when I open my eyes I see two white lines,

vertical, incandescent, I will keep all the knowledge

away I think, I try to think, I will keep

the knowing away, the lines seem to come out of nowhere,

they do not descend nor do they rise,
just gleam side by side in the small piece of glance
my two eyes hold in their close-up
vision. There is a flood. There are these two lines.
Then the sun moves up a notch, though still in the in-
visible, and I see, I see it is the 12-ounce glass, its body
illumined twice, white strokes where the very first
light has entered, here, I look again, it seems to gleam, it
gleams, it is the empty glass.

PRAYING (*Attempt of June 14 '03*)

This morning before dawn no stars I try again.

I want to be saved but from what. Researchers in California have

discovered a broken heart causes as much distress

in the pain center of the brain as physical injury.

The news was outside the door on the landing. I

squatted to it then came back in. Resume my

position. Knees tight, face pressed. There seems to be

a canyon. No light in it, yet it's there, but then

nothing. *Waste* comes

in, I know they are

burying our waste, that it will last hundreds of millions

of years in the mountain, that they are trying to cover it with signs they

do not know how to develop in

a language that will still communicate in that far

future saying don't open this, this is lethal beyond

measure, back away, go away, close the lid, close

the door. The canyons where my face lies full weight on the platter

of my hands have ridges and go forward only to

the buried waste. If there is beauty growing on those

flanks, beauty in detail—furred underside

of small desert leaves comes to mind but only as idea—

the sage twiggy stuff with its blue flowers—the succulent

floor plants that rise—the hundreds of crossing mucus-tracks on the walls where the

snails have been

guiding the first light

down their slick avenues to some core—all of it *just in*

mind not on my closed face trying

so hard to let the thing that can save us in—if

there is beauty it is missing in its manyness is only there

in form I am trying to be honest I am not relying on

chance any more I am trying to take matters

into my own hands. Hand heart head.

Brain pain center sleep. I try to

remember. Something that *was* once is not graspable

from here. Here is all here. Is the problem. Have

tucked the body away. Am all alone on this

floor. In a city in America. To make a

sacrifice. Of what. Save my beloveds. Save my

child. Save her right now. Destroy this carpeting these

windows the walls take the whole of what is wrong

in payment from us. Let me fall through the air.

Save the will to live, save the constituent part of

the human. No. What is constituent. Oh

save my child, my only child.

The more I press down onto the rug the more we move up the

canyon. In Mycenae we moved up this canyon too,

up, up through the city to the throne room at the top.

The columns still standing. The view of two oceans and over two

ranges. Where the King and his retinue are receiving the news. Here. The

poet ushered in. To sing of what has happened. Right here.

On this floor. The voice telling its story. Long, slow, in detail. All of them

waiting. Listening for the terrible outcome. In detail. The opening

of the singer at the throat. The still bodies of the

listeners, high on this outpost, 3,000 years ago, the house of

Agamemnon, the opening of the future. There. Right through the open

mouth of the singer. What happened, what

is to come. And the stillness surrounding them when it is done,

the song. And the singer still. And the chalices empty.

Dawn about to open it all up again. Dawn about to

move it from inside the mind back out. Light almost visible

on the far hills. Oh who will hear this. When it comes it will be time only for
action. Keep us in the telling I say face to the floor.
Keep us in the story. Do not force us back into the hell
of action, we only know how to kill. Once we stop singing we
only know how to get up and stride out of the room and begin
to choose, this from that, this from that, this from that,—and the pain,
the pain sliding into the folds of the brain and lodging.

Look, the steps move us up through the dark, I can hear them
even though I can't see them, we are moving further up,
this that this that and the pain sliding all along,
sliding into the fine crevices on the side walls of this brain we are
traveling up, and the pain lodging, and the pain finding the spot of
                                        unforgetting,

as in here I am, here I am.

IMPRESSIONISM

(Omaha Beach, 2001)

1.

Under her bonnet the silent little girl
in a white frock whose puffed-up sleeves sputter
                in the little
wind, whose also-white pinafore slaps its looping back-bow
this way and that against the landscape, stands
                very still,
on a small, arcing, quasi-ornamental bridge over the inlet streaming
                between dunes and land.
Sun shines down hard.
Everything seems to want to shout something out.
Beyond her, on that side, dune and tall dune grasses
                juggling long winds all one way
at any given once,
                made silvery by every mile-long bend.
She's leaning on the wooden rail. Her frock is jagged in its
                private wind
of starch and straightenings and cleanliness. Her hair
is held by tiny yellow bows.

2.

Downstream blue herons, two, wade in and fish.
Each beak catches the light a little differently.
Also, once, the foot uplifts in the isosceles

of just a single wading-step—half-interrupted now, as if mid-thought.

Look how it's held

as the eye discerns, among the currents, the half-truth that can

be caught.

3.

I feel these are the tablets of the law.
Midsummer, noon, grass, sand, surf, cloth.
Rectitude of birds. In-
candescent pinafore where she leans out over the

railing now.

The parked cars gleam. The streamlet gleams.
What is it one would listen past to hear?
Hands in my pockets I think of the holy tablets
again, trying to look everywhere at once.
What more am I supposed to do.
The bottom of things is neither life nor death.
The bottom is something else.

4.

As if a tree could siphon all its swollen fruit
back in, down into its limbs, dry up the

tiny opening

where manifestation slipped out—
taking it all back in—until it disappears—until
that's it: the empty tree with all inside it still—
versus this branching-out before me of *difference,* all

brilliantly lit, out-

reaching, variegating,

feeding a massive hunger.
The heron is full of hunger.

The miles of one-thought-driven grasses full of

                              hunger.

Although not in this register.

5.

I feel there is only one question.

Everywhere the shine covering the *through*

through which hunger must move.

And gladly. It must be done gladly or it

                        will not

serve. And yes there is surplus—

but on the surface (untouchable) and in the

                        narrow

(inaudible) we are slaves, ferrying the hunger back and

                                    forth.

6.

From the railing, down into the streambed,

a yellow string hangs from the fist of the

                        child—

crayon-yellow—fuzzy—with tiny filaments light lets us

                          see wind in.

It is repeated on the surface, then where it enters,

                        breaks.

Wind throbs sky, dress, grasses, about, but

the string's held taut by something underneath, so taut that very

close you'd hear the thrumming it is forced to make.

Perfect vertical! Calm fills me as I reach the

                        child.

What's on your string, I ask, arms full—towels, shoes, basket and

                                my book.

Where are the others is something that I also think—

also how full my head is of the wind,
papery, stripping my face away—hot dry woodplanks
                                        where my feet
are placed. Let it come on.
If I stand still I see
the shadow of the string on wood
grow shorter as it's drawn back up into
its source. Soon *something* will be here. I feel
consumer confidence: I laugh
out loud. A little wind.
Birdcheeping in the tall grass now.

                    7.

Swollen, thick, pin-cushioned-up with fat and slack-dead open
                                                    pores,
the bleached-out jumbo turkey-leg and thigh draws up
knotted to this yellow string—eleven crabs attached, all feeding
                                        wildly on their
                                        catch, clacking
their armors onto each other, claws embedded—pulled-up
                            by the yolk-
                            yellow force
onto the dock and crushed, each, at the head by the child's hammer
                                    taken to them
one by one—fast—only one scrambling across the bridge today
                            to get away—
the leg/thigh leaking all over the fading grayed-out planks,
the full-moon catch of crabs picked up claw-end by many
hands that seem to suddenly materialize
out of the nowhere to which I am
                now sent.
There's no way back believe me.
I'm writing you from there.

from

SEA CHANGE

SEA CHANGE

One day: stronger wind than anyone expected. Stronger than
                            ever before in the recording
                            of such. Un-
natural says the news. Also the body says it. Which part of the body—I look
                            down, can
                            feel it, yes, don't know
where. Also submerging us,
                            making of the fields, the trees, a cast of characters in an
                            unnegotiable
drama, ordained, iron-gloom of low light, everything at once undoing
                            itself. Also *sustained,* as in a hatred of
                            a thought, or a vanity that comes upon one out of
                            nowhere & makes
one feel the mischief in faithfulness to an
                            idea. Everything unpreventable and excited like
mornings in the unknown future. Who shall repair this now. And how the future
                            takes shape
                            too quickly. The permanent is ebbing. Is leaving
                            nothing in the way of
trails, they are blown over, grasses shoot up, life disturbing life, & it
                            fussing all over us, like a confinement gone
                            insane, blurring the feeling of
                            the state of
                            being. Which did exist just yesterday, calm and
true. Like the right to
                            privacy—how strange a feeling, here, the *right*—
                            consider your affliction says the

                              wind, do not plead ignorance, & farther and farther
                              away leaks the
past, much farther than it used to go, beating against the shutters I
                              have now fastened again, the huge mis-
                              understanding round me now so
                              still in
the center of this room, listening—oh,
                              these are not split decisions, everything
                              is in agreement, we set out willingly, & also knew to
                              play by rules, & if I say to you now
                              let's go
somewhere the thought won't outlast
                              the minute, here it is now, carrying its North
                              Atlantic windfall, hissing Consider
                              the body of the ocean which rises every instant into
                              me, & its
                              ancient e-
                              vaporation, & how it delivers itself
to me, how the world is our law, this indrifting of us
                              into us, a chorusing in us of elements, & how the
                              intermingling of us lacks in-
                              telligence, makes
reverberation, syllables untranscribable, in-clingings, & how wonder is also what
                              pours from us when, in the
                              coiling, at the very bottom of
                              the food
                              chain, sprung
from undercurrents, warming by 1 degree, the in-
                              dispensable
plankton is forced north now, & yet farther north,
                              spawning too late for the cod larvae hatch, such
that the hatch will not survive, nor the
                              species in the end, in the right-now forever un-

interruptible slowing of the

gulf

stream, so that I, speaking in this wind today, out loud in it, to no one, am suddenly

aware

of having written my poems, I feel it in

my useless

hands, palms in my lap, & in my listening, & also the memory of a season *at its*

full, into which is spattered like a

silly cry this in-

cessant leaf-glittering, shadow-mad, all over

the lightshafts, the walls, the bent back ranks of trees

all stippled with these slivers of

light like

breaking grins—infinities of them—wriggling along the walls, over the

grasses—mouths

reaching into

other mouths—sucking out all the

air—huge breaths passing to and fro between the unkind blurrings—& quicken

me further says this new wind, &

according to thy

judgment, &

I am inclining my heart towards the end,

I cannot fail, this Saturday, early pm, hurling myself,

wiry furies riding my many backs, against your foundations and your

best young

tree, which you have come outside to stake again, & the loose stones in the sill.

EMBODIES

Deep autumn & the mistake occurs, the plum tree blossoms, twelve

blossoms on three different

branches, which for us, personally, means none this coming spring or perhaps none on

just those branches on which

just now

lands, suddenly, a grey-gold migratory bird—still here?—crisping,

multiplying the wrong

air, shifting branches with small

hops, then stilling—very still—breathing into this oxygen which also pockets my

looking hard, just

that, takes it in, also my

thinking which I try to seal off,

my humanity, I was not a mistake is what my humanity thinks, I cannot

go somewhere

else than this body, the afterwards of each of these instants is just

another instant, breathe, breathe,

my cells reach out, I multiply on the face of

the earth, on the

mud—I can see my prints on the sweet bluish mud—where I was just

standing and reaching to see if

those really were blossoms, I thought perhaps paper

from wind, & the sadness in

me is that of forced parting, as when I loved a personal

love, which now seems unthinkable, & I look at

the gate, how open it is,

in it the very fact of God as

invention seems to sit, fast, as in its saddle, so comfortable—& where

does the road out of it

go—& are those torn wires hanging from the limbs—& the voice I heard once after I passed

what I thought was a sleeping

man, the curse muttered out, & the cage after they have let

the creatures

out, they are elsewhere, in one of the other rings, the ring with the empty cage is

gleaming, the cage is

to be looked at, grieving, for nothing, your pilgrimage ends here,

we are islands, we

should beget nothing &

what am I to do with my imagination—& the person in me trembles—& there is still

innocence, it is starting up somewhere

even now, and the strange swelling of the so-called Milky Way, and the sound of the

wings of the bird as it lifts off

suddenly, & how it is going somewhere precise, & that precision, & how I no longer

can say for sure that it

knows nothing, flaming, razory, the feathered serpent I saw as a child, of stone, &

how it stares back at me

from the height of its pyramid, & the blood flowing from the sacrifice, & the oracles

dragging hooks through the hearts in

order to say

what is coming, what is true, & all the blood, millennia, drained to stave off

the future, stave off,

& *the armies on the far plains,* the gleam off their armor now in this bird's

eye, as it flies towards me

then over, & the sound of the thousands of men assembled at

all cost now

the sound of the bird lifting, thick, rustling where it flies over—only see, it is

a hawk after all, I had not seen

clearly, it has gone to hunt in the next field, & the chlorophyll is

coursing, & the sun is

sucked in, & the chief priest walks away now where what remains of

the body is left

as is customary for the local birds.

GUANTÁNAMO

Waning moon. Rising now. Creak, it goes. Deep

over the exhausted continents. I wonder says my

fullness. Nobody nobody says the room in which I

lie very still in the

darkness watching. Your heart says the moon, waning & rising further. Where is it. Your

keep, your eyes your trigger

finger your spine your reasoning—also better to

refuse touch,

keep distance, let the blood run out of you and the white stars gnaw you, & the thorn

which is so white outside in the field,

& the sand which is sheetening on the long beach, the soldiers readying, the up-glance

swift when the key words, of prayer, before

capture, are

uttered, a shiver which has no hate but is not love, is neutral, yes, un-

blooded, as where for instance a bud near where

a hand is unlocking a

security-catch calls

out, & it is an instance of the nobody-there, & the sound of water darkens, & the wind

moves the grasses, & without

a cry the cold flows like a watchdog's

eyes, the watchdog keeping his eye out for difference—only difference—& acts being

committed in your name, & your captives arriving

at *your* detention center, there, in your

eyes, the lockup, deep in your pupil, the softening-up, you paying all your attention

out, your eyes, your cell, your keep, your hold,

after all it is yours, yes, what you have taken in, grasp it, grasp

this, there is no law, you are not open to

prosecution, look all you'd like, it will squirm for you, there, in this rising light, protected

from consequence, making you a

ghost, without a cry, without a cry the

evening turning to night, words it seemed were everything and then

the legal team will declare them exempt,

exemptions for the lakewater drying, for the murder of the seas, for the slaves in their

waters, not of our species, exemption named

go forth, mix blood, fill your register, take of flesh, set fire, posit equator, conceal

origin, say you are all forgiven, say these are only

counter-resistant coercive interrogation techniques, as in give me your

name, give it, I will take it, I will re-

classify it, I will withhold you from you, just like that, for a little while, it won't hurt

much, think of a garden, take your mind off

things, think sea, wind, thunder, root, think tree that will hold you

up, imagine it holding you

up, choose to be who you are, quick choose it, that will help. The moon is colder

than you think. It is full of nothing like

this stillness of ours. We are trying not to be noticed. We are in stillness as if it were an

other life we could slip into. In our skins

we dazzle with nonexistence. It is a trick of course but sometimes it works. If it

doesn't we will be found, we will be made to

scream and crawl. We will long to be forgiven. It doesn't matter for what, there are no

facts. Moon, who will write

the final poem? Your veil is flying, its uselessness makes us feel there is

still time, it is about two now,

you are asking me to lose myself.

In this overflowing of my eye,

I do.

LATER IN LIFE

Summer heat, the first early morning

    of it. How it lowers the pitch of the

    cry—human—cast up

as two words by the worker street-level

    positioning the long beam on

the chain as he calls up to the one handling the pulley on

    the seventh floor. One

    call. They hear each other!

Perfectly! As the dry heat, the filled-out leaves, thicken the surround, the warming

    asphalt, & the lull in growth

    occurs, & in it the single birdcries now and again

    are placed, &

all makes a round from which sound is sturdied-up without dissipation or dilation,

    bamboo-crisp, &

    up it goes up like a thing

    tossed without warp of weight or evidence of

    overcome

gravity, as if space were thinned by summer now to a non-interference. Up it goes, the

    cry, all the

    way up, audible and unchanging, so the man need

not even raise his voice to be heard,

    the dry warm air free to let it pass without

    loss of

    any of itself along

    its way. . . .

I step out and suddenly notice this: summer arrives, has arrived, is arriving. Birds grow

    less than leaves although they cheep, dip, arc. A call

across the tall fence from an invisible neighbor to his child is heard

                              right down to the secret mood in it the child

also hears. One hears in the silence that follows the great

                              desire for approval

                              and love

which summer holds aloft, all damp leached from it, like a thing floating out on a frail but

                              perfect twig-end. Light seeming to darken in it yet

                              glow. *Please* it says. But not with the eager need of

Spring! Come what may says summer. Smack in the middle I will stand and breathe. The

                              future is a superfluity I do not

                              taste, no, there is no numbering

here, it is a gorgeous swelling, no emotion, as in this love is no emotion, no, also no

                              memory—we have it all, now, & all

                              there ever was is

us, now, that man holding the beam by the right end and saying go on his

                              ground from

                              which the word and the

                              cantilevered metal

rise, there is no mistake, the right minute falls harmlessly, intimate, overcrowded,

                              without pro-

                              venance—perhaps bursting with nostalgia but

ripening so fast without growing at

                              all, & what

is the structure of freedom but this, & grace, & the politics of time—look south, look

                              north—yes—east west compile hope synthesize

exceed look look again hold fast attach speculate drift drift recognize forget—terrible

                              gush—gash—of

                              form of

outwardness, & it is your right to be so entertained, & if you are starting to

                              feel it is hunger this

                              gorgeousness, feel the heat fluctuate & say

                              my

                              name is day, of day, in day, I want nothing to

come back, not ever, & these words are mine, there is no angel to

wrestle, there is no inter-

mediary, there is something I must

tell you, you do not need existence, these words, praise be, they can for now be

said. That is summer. Hear them.

NEARING DAWN

Sunbreak. The sky opens its magazine. If you look hard

               it is a process of falling

               and squinting—& you are in-

terrupted again and again by change, & crouchings out there

               where you are told each second you

               are only visiting, & the secret

               whitening adds up to no

meaning, no, not for you, wherever the loosening muscle of the night

               startles-open the hundreds of

               thousands of voice-boxes, into which

your listening moves like an aging dancer still trying to glide—there is time for

               everything, everything, is there not—

               though the balance is

               difficult, is coming un-

done, & something strays farther from love than we ever imagined, from the long and

               orderly sentence which was a life to us, the dry

               leaves on

               the fields

through which the new shoots glow

               now also glowing, wet curled tips pointing in any

               direction—

as if the idea of a right one were a terrible forgetting—as one feels upon

               waking—when the dream is cutting loose, is going

               back in the other

direction, deep inside, behind, no, just back—&

               one is left looking out—& it is

breaking open further—what are you to do—how let it fully in—the wideness of it is staggering—you have to have more arms eyes a

thing deeper than laughter furrows more

capacious than hate forgiveness remembrance forgetfulness history silence

precision miracle—more

furrows are needed the field

cannot be crossed this way the

wide shine coming towards you standing in

the open window now, a dam breaking, reeking rich with the end of

winter, fantastic weight of loam coming into the

soul, the door behind you

shut, the

great sands behind there, the pharaohs, the millennia of carefully prepared and buried

bodies, the ceremony and the weeping for them, all

back there, lamentations, libations, earth full of bodies everywhere, our bodies,

some still full of incense, & the sweet burnt

offerings, & the still-rising festival out-cryings—& we will

inherit

from it all

nothing—& our ships will still go,

after the ritual killing to make the wind listen,

out to sea as if they were going to a new place,

forgetting they must come home yet again ashamed

no matter where they have been—& always the new brides setting forth—

& always these ancient veils of theirs falling from the sky

all over us,

& my arms rising from my sides now as if in dictation, & them opening out from me,

& me now smelling the ravens the blackbirds the small heat of the rot in this largest

cage—bars of light crisping its boundaries—

& look

there is no cover, you cannot reach

it, ever, nor the scent of last night's rain, nor the chainsaw raised to take the first of the

far trees

down, nor the creek's tongued surface, nor the minnow

turned by the bottom of the current—here

is an arm outstretched, then here

is rightful day and the arm still there, outstretched, at the edge of a world—tyrants

imagined by the bearer of the arm, winds listened for,

corpses easily placed anywhere the

mind wishes—inbox, outbox—machines

that do not tire in the

distance—barbed wire taking daysheen on—marking the end of the field—the barbs like a

lineup drinking itself

crazy—the wire

where it is turned round the post standing in for

mental distress—the posts as they start down the next field sorting his from

mine, his from the

other's—until you know, following,

following, all the way to the edge and then turning again, then again, to the

far fields, to the

height of the light—you know

you have no destiny, no, you have a wild unstoppable

rumor for a soul, you

look all the way to the end of

your gaze, why did you marry, why did you stop to listen,

where are your fingerprints, the mud out there hurrying to

the white wood gate, its ruts, the ants in it, your

imagination of your naked foot placed

there, the thought that in that there

is all you have & that you have

no rightful way

to live—

SUMMER SOLSTICE

Here it is now, emergent, as if an eagerness, a desire to say there this is

done this is

concluded I have given all I have the store

is full the

crop is

in the counsel has decided the head and shoulders of the invisible have been re-

configured sewn back together melded—the extra

seconds of light like

hearing steps come running towards me, then here you

are, you came all this

distance,

you could call it matrimony it is not an illusion it can be calculated to the last position,

consider no further think no longer all

art of

persuasion ends here, the head has been put back on the body, it stands before us

entire—it has been proven—all the pieces have

been found—the broken thing for an instant entire—oh strange

addition and sum, here is no other further step

to be taken, we have arrived, all the rest now a falling

back—but not yet not now now is all now and

here—the end of the day will not end—will stay with us

this fraction longer—

the hands of it all extending—

& where they would have turned away they wait,

there is nothing for now after this we shall wait,

shall wait that it reach us, this inch of finishing,

in what do you believe it leans out to suggest, slant,

as if to mend it the rip, the longest day of this one year,

not early and not late, un-

earned, unearnable—accruing to nothing, also to no one—how many more will I

see—no—wrong question—old question—how

strange that it be in

truth not now

conceivable, not as a thing-as-such, the personal death of

an I—& the extra millisecond adds itself to this day,

& learns, it too, to interline the cheek of light

given to the widening face

that stares at us holds us excels at

being—stands, dwells, purrs, allows—what can we say to it—standing in it—

quickly it arrives at full, no, not quickly, it

arrives, at fullest, then there it is, the

brim, where the fullness

stocks, pools, feeds, in-

dwells, is a

yes, I look up, I see your face through the window looking up,

see you bend to the

horizon-line,

do not myself look out at it, no, look at you,

at the long life of having-looked as a way of believing

now in your

thinking

face, & how natural the passage of time, and death, had felt to us, & how you

cannot

comprehend the thing you are meant

to be looking

for

now, & you are weighing something, you are out under the sky

trying to feel

the

future, there it is now in your almost invisible

squinting to the visible, & how I feel your heart beat slowly out there in the garden

        as we both see the

        dove

        in the

        youngest acacia,

& how it is making its nest again this year, how it chose the second ranking

        offshoot

again, how the young tree strains at the stake in the wind, & within,

        the still head of the mother sitting as if all time

        came down to

        this, the ringed neck, the

        mate's call from the

roof, & how we both know not to move—me inside at the window, deep summer, dusk,

        you in the line of sight of the

        bird, & also

        of the hawk changing sides of the field as

        usual,

& the swallows riding the lowest currents, reddish, seeking their feed.

ROOT END

The desire to imagine

the future.

Walking in the dark through a house you know by

heart. Calm. Knowing no one will be

out there.

Amazing

how you can move among

the underworld's

furniture—

the walls glide by, the desks, here a mirror sends back an almost unseeable

blink—a faraway lighthouse,

moonlessness—a planet going

out—here a

knotting of yet greater dark suggests

a door—a hollow feeling is a stair—the difference between

up and down a differential—so slight—of

temperature

and shift of provenance of

void—the side of your face

reads it—as if one could almost overhear laughter "down" there, birdcall "up" there—

although this is only an

analogy for different

silences—oh—

the mind knows our place so

deeply well—you could run through it—without fear—even in this total dark—this is what

the mind says in you: accelerate!—it is your

place, you belong, you know it by

heart, place—

not imaginable, nor under-

stood, where death is still an in-

dividual thing, & in the dark outside only the garden, & in each plant at core a thing

by

heart, & *after all these years* the heart says to itself each

beat, & look, if you make yourself think of it,

the roads out there will branch and branch then

vanish,

fanning out, flat, thinning away like root-ends, everywhere going only forward—&

so far from any so-called

city on the

hill, this city of dis-

appearance, root-ends then nothing, thinnest trailings of

all, forgiveness says the dark, smell

me breathe me in I am your inheritance forgive it,

dusk is already crushed tight and cannot be looked into

anymore, the glance between hunter and prey is choked off, under the big tent the

numbered rows grew

numberless long

ago, admittance is

free, as in you have

no choice, we are trying to block out the sound of drums in the distance, blessed be his

name says someone far in front at the

mike, & seats numbered 1 through 6 billion are

reserved, &

the story of the parted lovers, the one from the prior order,

will begin soon, you will see through the dark to it as it will

light itself

of its own accord,

also moonlight, what can filter through of it—&

look hard for where they rise and act, look hard to see

what action was—fine strength—it turns one inside out—

what is this growing inside of me, using me—such that the

wind can no longer blow through me—such that the dream in me grows cellular, then

muscular, my eyes red, my birth a thing I convey

beautifully

down this spiral staircase

made of words, made of

nothing but words—

THE VIOLINIST AT THE WINDOW, 1918

(after Matisse)

Here he is again, so thin, unbent, one would say captive—did winter ever leave—no one
has climbed the hill north of town in longer than one can remember—something hasn't
been fully loaded—life is blameless—he is a stem—& what here is cyclic, we would so

> need to know
>
> about now—& if there is
>
> a top to this—a summit, the highest note, a
>
> destination—

here he is now, again, standing at the window, ready to

> look out if asked to
>
> by his
>
> time,
>
> ready to take up again if he
>
> must, here where the war to end all wars has come
>
> to an end—for a while—to take up whatever it is
>
> the spirit

must take up, & what is the melody of

> that, the sustained one note of obligatory
>
> hope, taken in, like a virus,
>
> before the body grows accustomed to it and it
>
> becomes
>
> natural again—yes breathe it in,
>
> the interlude,
>
> the lull in the
>
> killing—up
>
> the heart is asked to go, up—

open these heavy shutters now, the hidden order of a belief system

                    trickles to the fore,

                    it insists you draw closer to

                    the railing—lean out—

time stands out there as if mature, blooming, big as day—& is this not an emaciated

                    sky, & how

                    thin is this

                    sensation of time, do you

not feel it, the no in the heart—no, do not make me believe

                    again, too much has died, do not make me open this

                    all up

                    again—crouching in

                    shadow, my head totally

                    empty—you can see

the whole sky pass through this head of mine, the mind is hatched and scored by clouds

                    and weather—what is weather—when it's

                    all gone we'll

                    buy more,

heaven conserve us is the song, & lakes full of leaping

                    fish, & ages that shall not end, dew-drenched, sun-

                    drenched, price-

                    less—leave us alone, loose and undone, everything

and nothing slipping through—no, I cannot be reached, I cannot be duped again says

                    my head standing now in the

                    opened-up window, while history starts up again, &

                    is that flute music in the

distance, is that an answering machine—call and response—& is that ringing in my ears

                    the furrows of earth

                    full of men and their parts, & blood as it sinks into

loam, into the page of statistics, & the streets out there, shall we really

                    be made to lay them out again, & my plagiarized

                    humanity, whom

                    shall I now imitate to re-

                    become

before the next catastrophe—the law of falling bodies applies but we shall not use

it—the law of lateness—

even our loved ones don't know if we're living—

but I pick it up again, the

violin, it is

still here

in my left hand, it has been tied to me all this long time—I shall hold it, my

one burden, I shall hear the difference between up

and

down, & up we shall bring the bow now up &

down, & find

the note, sustained, fixed, this is what hope forced upon oneself by one's self sounds

like—this high note trembling—it is a

good sound, it is an

ugly sound, my hand is doing this, my mind cannot

open—cloud against sky, the freeing of my self

from myself, the note is that, I am standing in

my window, my species is ill, the

end of the world can be imagined, minutes run away like the pattering of feet in summer

down the long hall then out—oh be happy, &

clouds roil, & they hide the slaughterhouse, they loft as if this were

not

perpetual exile—we go closer—the hands at the end of this body

feel in their palms

the great

desire—look—the instrument is raised—

& this will be a time again in which to *make*—a time of use-

lessness—the imagined human

paradise.

FUTURES

Midwinter. Dead of. I own you says my mind. Own what, own

                whom. I look up. Own the looking at us

say the cuttlefish branchings, lichen-black, moist. Also

                the seeing, which wants to feel more than it sees.

Also, in the glance, the feeling of owning, accordioning out and up,

                seafanning,

& there is cloud on blue ground up there, & wind which the eye loves so deeply it

                would spill itself out and liquefy

                to pay for it—

& the push of owning is thrilling, is spring before it

                is—is that swelling—is the imagined fragrance as one

bends, before the thing is close enough—wide-

                eyed leaning—although none of this can make you

                happy—

because, looking up, the sky makes you hear it, you know why we have come it

                blues, you know the trouble at the heart, blue, blue, what

pandemonium, blur of spears roots cries leaves master & slave, the crop destroyed,

                water everywhere not

                drinkable, & radioactive waste in it, & human bodily

waste, & what,

                says the eye-thinking heart, is the last color seen, the last word

heard—someone left behind, then no behind—

                is there a skin of the I own which can be scoured from inside the

                glance—no,

                cannot—& always

                someone walking by whistling a

                little tune, that's

life he says, smiling, there, that was life—& the heart branches with its

wild arteries—I own my self, I own my

leaving—the falcon watching from the tree—I shall torch the crop that no one else

have it whispers the air—

& someone's swinging from a rope, his rope—the eye

throbbing—day a noose looking for a neck—

the fire spidery but fast—& the idea of

friends, what was that, & the day, in winter, your lower back

started acting up again, & they pluck out the eyes at the end for

food, & don't forget

the meeting at 6, your child's teacher

wishes to speak to you

about his future, & if there is no food and the rain is everywhere switching-on as expected,

& you try to think of music and the blue of Giotto,

& if they have to eat the arms he will feel no pain at least, & there is a

sequence in which feeding takes

place—the body is owned by the hungry—one is waiting

one's turn—one wants to own one's

turn—and standing there,

don't do it now but you might remember kisses—how you kissed his arm in the sun

and

tasted the sun, & this is your

address now, your home address—& the strings are cut no one

looks up any longer

—or out—no—&

one day a swan appeared out of nowhere on the drying river,

it

was sick, but it floated, and the eye felt the pain of rising to take it in—I own you

said the old feeling, I want

to begin counting

again, I will count what is mine, it is moving quickly now, I will begin this

message "I"—I feel the

smile, put my hand up to be sure, yes on my lips—the yes—I touch it again, I begin counting, I say *one* to the swan, *one,*

do not be angry with me o my god, I have begun the action of beauty again, on

the burning river I have started the catalogue,

your world,

I your speck tremble remembering money, its dry touch, sweet strange

smell, it's a long time, the smell of it like lily of the valley

sometimes, and pondwater, and how

one could bend down close to it

and drink.

UNDATED LULLABY

I go out and there she is still of course sitting on the nest, dead-center in-
                                          visible in our flowing big-
                                          headed
still young and staked acacia, crown an almost
                                          perfect
                                          circle, dark greens blurring now
in this high wind, wrestling it, compliant too—billion-mouthed transformer of
                                          sun and the carbon molecule—
                                          & you have to stand still and
                                          look in to see her,
there where the wind splits open the head, slashes the branches, & you see her,
                                          & her head does not even turn or
                                          tuck—
heart, jewel, bloom, star—not on any rung as we are on rungs—I can't help but
                                          look,
                                          wind-slicings keep
                                          revealing her, felt-still, absorbent of
light, sound, gaze, idea—I have seen everything bought and sold I think—
                                          the human heart is a
                                          refugee—is standing here always in
                                          its open
                                          market, shouting out prices, in-
audible prices, & wares keep on arriving, & the voices get higher—
                                          what are you worth the map of the world is
shrieking, any moment of you, what is it
                                          worth, time breaks over you and you
                                          remain, more of you, more of you,

asking your questions, ravishing the visible with your inquiry, and hungry, why are you
                              so hungry, you have already been
                              fed, close your
mouth, close your neck, close your hands chest mind, close them   & your eyes,
                              close them—make arrangements to hold
                              yourself together, that will be needed, make of your
                              compassion a
crisper instrument, you will need its blade, you will need
                              bitterness, stand here all you like looking in, you
                              will need to learn
                              to live in this prison
                              of blood and breath,
                              & the breeze passes by so generously, & the air
has the whole earth in its mind and it thinks it, thinks it, & in the corner of your cell
                              look carefully, you are of the ones who worship
cruelty—looking in to her nest, the bloom which is your heart opens with
                              kindness,
you can feel it flow through you as your eyes take her
                              in—strange sweetness this—high note—held—
but it is in your hands you must look
                              for the feeling of what is human,
                              and in your palms feel
what the tall clouds on the horizon oar-in to you—what will forever replace
                              stillness of mind—
look out for them their armada is not aware of your air-conditioned
                              office—swimmingly the thunderheads arrive &
                              when
is the last time you cried out loud, & who are those there
                              still shuffling through their files,
                              trying to card-out what to shred
                              in time, &
are you still giving out character references, to
                              whom, & the tickets, who paid for them this

time—your

voice, was it raised too high for the

circumstance—were you too

visible,

did you make sufficient progress, is the address still in your pocket, who paid, who left

the tip, the garden, the

love, the thirst—oh who

was so hungry they ate of the heaven, they ate the piece of it, they ripped its

seam—look the stitching is coming

undone—moon, river-in-the-

distance, stars above the tree, wind dying down—why are you

still here—the end of evening has *come*

and gone—crammed to its full with the whole garden and its creatures—why

are you still here, your eyes like mouths—shut them now—&

tuck in your pleasure, tuck it in,

move on into the deeper water, your kind

await you, sprawling in their camps,

longing to be recognized,

& the harsh priest the cold does his nightly round,

& the huge flower of reason blooms, blooms,

& somebody has a newspaper, not today's, no, but some day's,

and if you can find a corner,

you can pick it up—ignoring the squint-eyed girl, the sensation of

falling, the general theory of

relativity, the nest of

meaning—you can sit in your exile

and, to the tune of the latest song, the recording of what was at some moment the song

of the moment, the *it* song, the thing

you couldn't

miss—it was everywhere—everyone was singing it—you can find your

mind

and in the firelight

catch up on that distant moment's news.

NO LONG WAY ROUND

Evening. Not quite. High winds again.

        I have time, my time, as you also do, there, feel

        it. And a heart, my heart, as you do,

remember it. Also am sure of some things, there are errands, this was a voyage, one

        has an ordained part to play. . . . This will turn out to be

        not true

but is operative here for me this evening as the dusk settles. One has to believe

        furthermore in the voyage of others. The dark

        gathers. It is advancing but there is no

progress. It is advancing with its bellyful of minutes. It seems to chew as it

        darkens. There was, in such a time, in addition,

an obligation to what we called telling

        the truth. We

        liked

        the feeling

        of it—truth—whatever we meant by it—I can still

feel it in my gaze, tonight, long after it is gone, that finding of all the fine discriminations,

        the edges, purse holding the goods, snap shut, there,

you got it, there, it is yours it is true—hold onto it as

        light thins

        holding the lavender in its heart, firm, slow, beginning to

hide it, to steal it, to pretend it never had

        existence. At the window, I stand spell-

bound. Your excellency the evening, I begin. What is this trickiness. I am passing

        through your checkpoint to a nation that is

disappearing, is disappearance. My high-ceilinged room (I look

        up) is only going to evade

invisibility

for the while longer we

have the means

to keep it. I look at the pools of light in it. The carpet shining-up its weave—

burgundy, gold, aqua, black. It is an emergency actually, this waking and doing and

cleaning-up afterwards, & then sleep again, & then up you go, the whole 15,000 years of

the inter-

glacial period, & the orders & the getting done &

the getting back in time & the turning it back on, & did you remember, did you pass, did

you lose the address again, didn't the machine spit it up, did you follow the machine—

yes, yes, did, & the

wall behind it

pronounced the large bush then took it

back. I can almost summon it. Like changing a tense. I peer back through this time to

that one. You will not believe it

when the time

comes. Also how we mourned our dead—had

ample earth, took time, opened it, closed

it—"our earth, our

dead" we called

them, & lived

bereavement, & had strict understandings of defeat and victory. . . . Evening,

what are the betrayals that are left,

and whose? I ask now

as the sensation of what is coming places its shoulders on the whole horizon, I see it

though it is headless, intent

fuzzy, possible outcomes

unimaginable. You have your imagination, says the evening. It is all you have

left, but its neck is open, the throat is

cut, you have not forgotten how to sing, or to want

to sing. It is

strange but you still

need to tell

your story—how you met, the coat one wore, the shadow of which war, and how it lifted,

and how peace began again

for that part of

the planet, & the first Spring after your war, & how "life" began again, what

normal was—thousands of times

you want to say this—normal—holding another's

hand—& the poplars when you saw how much they had grown while you were

away—

the height of them! & the paper lantern you were

given to hold—the lightness of it, of its

fire, how it lit the room—it was your room—you were alone in it and free to sleep

without worry and to

dream—winter outside and the embroidered tablecloth—fruit and water—you didn't
even wonder where was the tree that gave such fruit, you lay in blankets as if they were
non-existent, heat was a given, the rain coming down hard now, what a nice sound—you
could ruminate, the mind traveled back in those days, at ease, it recalled the evening's
con-

versation, the light that fell on x's face, how he
turned when a certain person entered the room—you saw him turn—saw shyness then
jealousy enter his eyes as he looked away—and did he see you see him—and the em-
broidered linen handkerchief you saw a frightened woman in the subway slide from her
pocket, use and replace—then sleep was near—somewhere you were a child and then this
now, nightfall and ease, hospitality—

there are sounds the planet will always make, even

if there is no one to hear them.

from

PLACE

SUNDOWN

(St. Laurent Sur Mer, June 5, 2009)

Sometimes the day

        light winces

        behind you and it is

a great treasure in this case today a man on

        a horse in calm full

        gallop on Omaha over my

        left shoulder coming on

        fast but

calm not audible to me at all until I turned back my

        head for no

        reason as if what lies behind

        one had whispered

what can I do for you today and I had just

        turned to

        answer and the answer to my

answer flooded from the front with the late sun he/they

        were driving into—gleaming—

        wet chest and upraised knees and

light-struck hooves and thrust-out even breathing of the great

        beast—from just behind me,

        passing me—the rider looking straight

        ahead and yet

smiling without looking at me as I smiled as we

        both smiled for the young

        animal, my feet in the

breaking wave-edge, his hooves returning, as they begin to pass

        by,

        to the edge of the furling

        break, each tossed-up flake of

        ocean offered into the reddish

luminosity—sparks—as they made their way,

        boring through to clear out

        life, a place where no one

        again is suddenly

killed—regardless of the "cause"—no one—just this

        galloping forward with

        force through the low waves, seagulls

        scattering all round, their

screeching and mewing rising like more bits of red foam, the

        horse's hooves now suddenly

        louder as it goes

        by and its prints on

wet sand deep and immediately filled by thousands of

        sandfleas thrilled to the

declivities in succession in the newly

        released beach—just

        at the right

        moment for some

microscopic life to rise up through these

        cups in the hard upslant

        retreating ocean is

revealing, sandfleas finding them just as light does,

        carving them out with

        shadow, and glow on each

        ridge, and

water oozing up through the innermost cut of the

        hoofsteps,

and when I shut my eyes now I am not like a blind person

                    walking towards the lowering sun,

the water loud at my right,

                    but like a seeing person

with her eyes shut

                    putting her feet down

                    one at a time

                    on the earth.

CAGNES SUR MER 1950

I am the only one who ever lived who remembers

my mother's voice in the particular shadow

cast by the skyfilled Roman archway

which darkens the stones on the down-sloping street

up which she has now come again suddenly.

How the archway and the voice and the shadow

seize the small triangle of my soul

violently, as in a silent film where the accompaniment

becomes a mad body

for the spirit's skipping images—abandoned homeland—miracle from which

we come back out alive. So here from there again I,

read it off the book of time,

my only time, as if in there is a fatal mistake of which

I cannot find the nature—or shape—or origin—I

pick up the infant and place it back again

to where I am a small reservoir of blood, twelve pounds of bone and

sinew and other matters—already condemned to this one soul—

which we are told weighs less than a feather, or as much

as four ounces when grown—as if I could travel, I back up

those arteries, up the precious liquid, across the field of methods, agonies,

astonishments—may I not squander the astonishments—

may I not mistakenly kill brother, sister—I

will sit once again so boldly at my beginning,

dark spot where one story does not yet become another,

and words, which have not yet come to me, will not yet try to tell

where each thing emerges, where it is heading,

and where the flow of tendency will shine

on its fast way downhill. And it will seem to me

that all this is legend,

one of those in which there is no way to look back

and yet you do, you pay for it, yes, but you do. . . .

It was a hilltop town in the south in summer.

It was before I knew about knowing.

My mind ran everywhere and was completely still at the center.

And that did not feel uncomfortable.

A bird sang, it added itself to the shadow

under the archway.

I think from this distance

that I was happy.

I think from this distance.

I sat. It was before I knew walking.

Only my soul walked everywhere without weight.

Where the road sloped downhill there was disappearance.

Which was exactly what I imagined should happen.

Appearance and disappearance.

In my only life.

When my mother's voice got closer it had a body.

It had arms and they were holding something

that must have been a basket. My mind now

can go round her, come in front, and wrap her

as her arms wrapped that basket.

And it must have been wicker

because I see in the light the many lucent browns, the white tips,

as she steps out of the shadow

in which nothing but her hands and the front of her act of carrying

are visible. And when her body arrives

it is with the many lemons entirely struck, entirely taken, by sunshine,

which the heavy basket is still now carrying,

and her bright fingernails woven into each other,

and her face with its gaze searching for me,

gaze which felt like one of the bright things she was carrying

in front of herself, a new belly.

All I was to invent in this life is there in the wicker basket among the lemons

having come from below the horizon where the sound of the market rises

up into the private air in which she is moving,

where she is still a whole woman, and a willing woman,

and I hear what must be prices and names called out

of flowers and fruit and meat and live animals in small cages,

all from below us, at the bottom of the village, from that part

which is so comfortable to me which is invisible,

and in which everything has to be sold by noon.

I think that was the moment of my being given my name,

where I first heard the voices carrying the prices

as her face broke and its smile appeared bending down towards me

saying *there you are, there you are.*

ON THE VIRTUE OF THE DEAD TREE

And that you hold the same one hawk each day I pass through my field
up. And that it
may choose its
spot so
freely, from which to scan, and, without more than the wintry beguiling
wingstrokes seeding
the fields of air,
swoop. It feeds. There is no wasteland where the dead oak
lives—my
darling—up-
start vines on its trunk, swirling in ebblight, a desert of gone-silent
cells—where another force is
gleaming—tardy—
waning—summer or winter no longer
truths, no prime, no
year, no day where sun
exists—
just a still-being-here in this small apparently silent multitudinous world of
infinite yearning and
killing and
sprouting—even now at the very start of the season—lengthening, in-
visible in their
cracking open of
pod—and push—like the first time we saw each other you and I—
impatient immediately . . .
Blackness is the telephone wire—blackness the blissless instant-
communication,

the twittering poverty killing behind and beneath and deep at the core of

each screen, end-

less, someone breaking someone's

fingers—just now—hear their laughter—everyone in their prison—there in their human

heart which

they cannot

for all the parting of flesh with

cement-sluiced rubber

hose—and even the axe to the heart—reach—the fantasy of independence—es-

cape. It wants them. It wants them to

fly inside it. *Fly* it screams

taser in

hand. Prison is never

going to be

over. Day as it breaks is the principal god, but with the hood on they cannot

know this. Till it is finally sliced open the

beating heart. Loved

ones shall pay

ransom

for the body of

their child. To this, friend, the hero is the dead tree. Here in my field, mine.

I have forced it. I have paid for it. My money like a wind flowing over it.

Have signed the paperwork and seen my name there. And a cloud

arrives from the East

into it. And the prison

grows too large to see.

And it does not sing, ever,

my silent hawk, always there when I arrive, before it startles, on its chosen

branch. And I think of

the dead-through trunk, the leafless limbs, the loosening of the

deep-drying roots in the

living soil. And I slow myself to extend love to them. To their as-

yet-still-sturdy

rotting, and how they hold

up this gray-blue

poverty of once-sapflowing

limbs, their once everywhere-turning

branchings,

for my small hungry creature to glide from in his silence

over the never-for-an-instant-not-working

rows of new

wheat. It is

good says my human soul to the crop. I will not listen for

song anymore. I will

listen for how dark comes-on to loosen the cringing wavering

mice from their dens and

how they creep up to the surfaces and out onto the surfaces and

how the surfaces

yield their small gray velvet barely visible in the last glow

to that part of the world

the dead tree sends forth. I have lived I

say to the evening.

I have plenty of anger and am good and dry with late-breaking news. I

am living.

And the iron door of the night creeps and clicks. And the

madness of the day

hangs around restless at the edges of the last visible leaves

with a reddish glow

and moves them with tiny

erratic swiftnesses and

the holy place shuts, baggy with evening, and here it is

finally night

bursting open

with hunt.

THE BIRD ON MY RAILING

From
$\qquad$ the still wet iron of
$\qquad$ my fire
$\qquad$ escape's top
railing a truth is making this instant on our clock
$\qquad$ open with a taut
$\qquad$ unchirping un-
$\qquad$ breaking note—a perfectly
$\qquad$ released vowel traveling
the high branches across the way, between us and the
$\qquad$ others, in their
$\qquad$ apartments, and fog
lifting for sun before evaporation
$\qquad$ begins. Someone
$\qquad$ is born
$\qquad$ somewhere
$\qquad$ now. The
$\qquad$ planet
$\qquad$ suspends
$\qquad$ like a streetlight
$\qquad$ at night
$\qquad$ in the quiet
$\qquad$ galaxy.
$\qquad$ Endurance
continues to be the secret of the tilled
$\qquad$ ground we make
$\qquad$ breath by breath. What

                              seed dear

                              lord are we we

think as we toss more of our living out

                              into the turning and turning,

                              our personal

dead cast always deeper into

                              the general dead

                              no matter how hard you try

                              to keep your

                              own your

known own—and gnarled remembering mossing over—

                              the tenderness a characteristic trait

                              elicits, the very thing you

                              hated, rising in you to

                              make you almost

                              unable to

                              speak—

—where *are* you?—the fields beyond the housing tract

                              still accepting rain

                              as these asphalted ones we've

                              sealed

cannot—so yes, look close, this right word on my railing

                              who knows no hate

                              no love

                              you can count on it,

no wrenching strangling guilt, no wish so terrible

                              one had said

                              otherwise just once in

                              time—

between one life and another what is it that

                              can really

                              exist—oh

                              nothing says this

awakeness—and look, you

who might not believe this because

you are not seeing it with your own

eyes: look:

this light

is moving

across that flower on

my sill

at this exact

speed—right now—right here—now it is gone—yet go back up

five lines it is

still there I can't

go back, it's

gone,

but you—

what is it you are

seeing—see it again—a yellow

daisy, the sun

strafing the petals once

across, and the yellow, which could be a god why not,

pulling itself up

out of

shadow—so

silent—

and the patch of sunlight

moves—and each word said in

time after this is

the subtraction we call

life-lived—this gold its center—and beyond it, still on

the rail, this

bird, a

secret gift to

me by the

visible—

of which few in a life are

       given—and how

       when it opens its

       yellow beak in the glint-sun to

       let out song

       into the cold, it

lets out the note on a plume of

       steam,

       lets out the

       visible heat of its

       inwardness

carrying a note—a note in

       a mist—a note-

       breath, breath-

       note—oh

cold spring—the white

       plume the size of a

       bird rises up with its own

       tail,

       feathering-out in

the directions,

       filled out by the next and the next-on

       note, until the whole

       shape of the

       song is wisped-

       up and

shuts,

       the singing

       shuts, the form

       complete, the breath-bird

       free to

       rise away into the young day and

not be—

THE BIRD THAT BEGINS IT

In the world-famous night which is already flinging away bits of dark but not

        quite yet

        there opens

        a sound like a

        rattle, then a slicing in which even the

        blade is

audible, and then again, even though trailing the night-melt, suddenly, again, the

        rattle. In the

night of the return of day, of next-on time, of

        shape name field

        with history flapping

        all over it

invisible flags or wings or winds—(*victory* being exactly

        what it says,

        the end of night)

(it is not right to enter time it mutters as its tatters

        come loose)—in the

        return I

        think *I*

        am in this body—

I really only think it—this body lying here is

        only my thought,

        the flat solution

        to the sensation/question

        of

who is it that is listening, who is it that is wanting still

        to speak to you

out of the vast network

of blooded things,

a huge breath-held, candle-lit, whistling, planet-wide, still blood-flowing,

howling-silent, sentence-driven, last-bridge-pulled-up-behind city of

the human, the expense-

column of place in

place humming. . . . To have

a body. A borderline

of ethics and reason. Here comes the first light in leaf-shaped coins.

They are still being flung at our feet. We could be Judas no

problem. Could be

the wishing-well. Right

here in my open

mouth. The light can toss its wish right down this spinal

cord,

can tumble in

and buy a wakened self. . . . What is the job today my being

asks of

light. Please

tell me my job. It cannot be this headless incessant crossing

of threshold, it cannot be

more purchasing of more

good, it cannot be more sleeplessness—the necklaces of

minutes being tossed

over and over my

shoulders. The snake

goes further into the grass as

first light hits.

The clay

in the soil gleams where dew withdraws. Something we don't want

any more of

flourishes as never

before. I

feel the gravity

as I sit up

like a leaf growing from the stalk of the unknown

still lying there behind me where my sleep just was. Daylight

crackles on the sill. Preparation

of day

everywhere

underfoot. Across

the sill, the hero unfolding in the new light, the

girl who would

not bear the

god a

son, the mother who ate her own grown

flesh, the god

who in exchange

for Time gave as many of his children as need be

to the

abyss. It is

day.

The human does not fit in it.

END

(November 21, 2010)

End of autumn. Deep fog. There are chains in it, and sounds of
                              hinges. No that was
                              birds. A bird and a
                              gate. There are
swingings of the gate that sound like stringed
                              instruments from
                              some other
                              culture. Also a
hammering which is held
                              in the fog
                              and held. Or it is continuing to
                              hammer. I hear the blows.
Each is distant so it seems it should not repeat. It repeats. What is it being hammered
                              in. Fog all over the
                              field. The sounds of
                              boots
on soil in groups those
                              thuds but then it is
                              cattle I
                              think. The sound of the hinge the swinging chain it won't
go away. But it is just the farmer at work. He must be putting out
                              feed. Fog. Play at
                              freedom now it

                    says, look, all is

                    blank. Come to the

                    front, it is

                    your stage it

                    says, the sound of the clinking of links of

chain, I think it is someone making the chain—*that* is the hammering—the thuds—making
their own chain. But no, it is the gate and the herd is let in again, then

                    out. I can hear

the mouths eating, dozens maybe hundreds, and the breathing in and out as they

                    chew. And the

                    chain. For now I am alive I think into the hammering

thudding clinking swinging of metal hinge—of hinge—and also think maybe this is
winter now—first day of. Fog and a not knowing of. Of what. What is inner

                    experience I think being

                    shut out. I look. A gate swings again and a rustling

                    nearby. All is

nearby and invisible. The clinking a chinking of someone making nails. The sounds of a crowd
meaning to be silent, all their breathing. Having been told not to move and to be

                    silent. Then having been told to

                    move and be

                    silent. The crowd is in there. All the breaths they are trying

                    to hold in, make

inaudible. And scraping as of metal on metal, and dragging as of a heavy thing. But it is a field
out there. My neighbor has his herd on it. When I walk away from the

                    window it's a violin I

                    hear over the

                    chewing out of tune torn string but once it made

                    music it might still make

                    music if I become a new way of

                    listening, in which

                    above all,

                    nothing, I know nothing, now there are moans

out there such as a man accused and tossed away by his fellow beings, an aloneness, and
listen, it is blank but in it is an
appeal, a ruined one, reduced, listen: in
there this
animal
dying slowly
in eternity its
trap.

EMPLOYMENT

Listen the voice is American it would reach you it has wiring in its swan's neck

where it is

always turning

round to see behind itself as it has no past to speak of except some nocturnal

journals written in woods where the fight has just taken place or is about to

take place

for place

the pupils have firelight in them where the man a surveyor or a tracker still has

no idea what

is coming

the wall-to-wall cars on the 405 for the ride home from the cubicle or the corner

office—how big

the difference—or the waiting all day again in line till your number is

called it will be

called which means

exactly nothing as no one will say to you as was promised by all eternity "ah son, do you

know where you came from, tell me, tell me your story as you have come to this

Station"—no, they

did away with

the stations

and the jobs

the way of

life

and your number, how you hold it, its promise on its paper,

if numbers could breathe each one of these would be an

exhalation, the last breath of something

and then there you have it: stilled: the exactness: the number: your number. That is why they

can use it. Because it was living

and now is

stilled. The transition from one state to the

other—they

give, you

receive—provides its shape.

A number is always hovering over something beneath it. It is

invisible, but you can feel it. To make a sum

you summon a crowd. A large number is a form

of mob. The larger the number the more

terrifying.

They are getting very large now.

The thing to do right

away

is to start counting, to say it is my

turn, mine to step into

the stream of blood

for the interview,

to say I

can do it, to say I

am not

one, and then say two, three, four and feel

the blood take you in from above, a legion

single file heading out in formation

across a desert that will not count.

TREADMILL

The road keeps accepting us. It wants us to learn "nowhere," its shiny

        emptiness, its smile of wide days, so swollen

with void, it really means it, this is not a vacation, it wants us

        to let our skulled-in mind, its channels and runnels, its

        slimy stalked circuits, connecting wildly, it the road

        wants us

        right now

        to cast it the

        mind

        from its encasement

        forward

to race up ahead and get a feel for what it is, this always-receding, this place in which

        you were to deposit your

        question—the

        destination!—the mind is meant to want this, isn't it,

        meant to rage to

        handle it, to turn it

        round, to feel

        all its

        facets—its fine

        accidents—death by water, death by

wearing out—death by surprise—death by marriage—death by having rummaged

into the past, into the distant past—death by ice-core and prediction—the entrails are lying on a

thousand years of tabletops—have you not looked into them enough says the grayish

        road, hissing, or maybe

        that is my mind, I

        entered the poem here,

on line 28, at 6:44 pm, I had been trying to stay outside, I had not wanted to

put my feet here too, but the wind came up, a little achilles-wind, the city itself took

time off from dying to whisper into my ear we need you, the complaint which we will

nail once again to the door must be signed by everyone, everyone needs to be walking

together, everyone must feel the dust underfoot, death by drought, death by starvation,

death by neglect, death by no cause of death, by unfolding—oh the rose garden—

dew still on it, the dry fields in each drop held up by the petal—look you can see

the cracks in the soil reflected right there—puritanical dried fields—sincerity at utmost

in the fissured field—the screen is empty—is full of cracked soil—the soil—

death by transcendent truth—death by banking practice—by blueprint and mutually

assured destruction—death by deterrent—detergent—derangement—defamation—de-

regulation—the end of the line—where the tracks just stop and

who is that coming from the woodshed to greet you—the end is always cheerful

                    says the day hurrying alongside as you splice

                    through it, as you

                    feel your astonishing aloneness grow funnily

                    winged—who are you going to be

someday, who are you going to be when all this clay flowing through you has

                    finally become

                    form, and you catch a glimpse of yourself at daybreak,

                    there in the shiny broken-faced

                    surface—

who was awaiting you all day that you hurried so—what was it you were told to

                    accomplish—death, rimless stare, O, hasn't enough time

passed by now, can the moving walkway be shut down for the night, but no,

                    it is told, it is told, the universe

                    is in your mind as it

                    expands—and it is October once again

as it must be, the new brightness—

                    and again gold lays down on them

                    the tight rolls of hay,

                    the long rows the cut fields—

which Winter eyes, hidden as it is at the core of everything, and the crows sharpen their blade-calls on the morning,

and frost blooms its parallel world,

and the road seems to want to be spooled into your hands, into your mind, fine

yarn you would ravel

back to its place of

origin—

is it true some people are not coming along with us? is it really true there is

a road not taken? and it is October once again

as it must be, the new brightness, the harvest—the dance—

and your dance partner, be prudent, it

really knows the

steps.

DIALOGUE
(OF THE IMAGINATION'S FEAR)

All around in

              houses near us, the

              layoffs,

              the windows shine back

              sky, it is a

              wonder we

can use the word *free* and have it mean anything at all

              to us. We stand still. Let the cold wind wrap round go

              into hair in-

between fingers. The *for sale* signs are bent and ripple in

              wind. One

had fallen last Fall and snowmelt is re-revealing

              it again. Rattle in groundwind. Siding

              weakening on

              everything. Spring!

              Underneath

              the bulbs want to clear the sill of

              dark and find the

              sun. I see

              them now

under there, in there, soggy with melt, and loam which is loosening as their skins

rot, to let the whitest tendrils out, out they go snaking everywhere, till the

              leaves are blurring, they fur-out, they

              exist!—

              another's year loan

              to time—

and the bud will form in the sleeve of the silky leaf, and they will quietly,
among the slow working pigeons and there where a dog is leaping in almost
                              complete invisibility, make slim heads,
                              thicken—I am ill, you know, says the man walking by,
his dog pulling him, so much joy, and nothing
                              will make it more or less, the flower,
as alive as it is dead, above which the girl with earphones walks humming, no one
                              has warned her yet she is
                              free, but why, says the
                              imagination, have you sent me
                              down here, down among the roots, as they finally take
hold—it is hard—they wrench, the loam is not easy to open, I cannot say it but the
smell is hope meeting terrifying regret, I would say do not open again, do not go up,
                              stay under here there is
                              no epoch, we are
                              in something but it is not "the world," why try to make
                              us feel at
                              home down
                              here, take away the poem, take away this desire that
has you entering this waste dark space, there are not even pockets of time here,
there are no mysteries, there is no laughter and nothing ever dies, the foreclosure
                              you are standing beside look to it, there is a
woman crying on the second floor as she does not understand what it will be like to
not have a home now, and how to explain to the children at 3:35 when the bus drops
                              them off—
the root is breaking its face open and shoving up to escape
                              towards
                              sun—nothing can stop it—though right
now the repo-men have not yet come, the school bus is only just getting loaded up,
the children pooling squealing some stare out the window. Kiss
                              the soil as you
pass by. It is coming up to kiss you. Bend down to me, you have placed me here, look
to me on all fours, drink of the puddle, look hard at the sky in there. It is not sky. It is

not there. The flame of

sun which will come out just now for a blinding minute

into your eyes is saving nothing, no one, take your communion, your blood is full of

barren fields, they are the

future in you you

should learn to feel and

love: there will be no more: no more: not enough to go around: no more around: no

more: love that.

LULL

At the forest's edge, a fox

                came out.

                It looked at

us. Nobody coming up the hill hungry looking

                to take

                food. The fox-

                eye

trained. Nobody coming up the

                hill in the broad

                daylight with an

                axe for

wood, for water, for the store in the

                pantry. I stock

                the pantry. I

watch for rain. For too much

                rain, too

                fast, too

                little, too

long. When dryness begins I hear the woods

                click. Unusual.

                I hear the arid. Un-

                usual. My father

                is dying of

age, good, that is usual. My valley is,

                my touch, my sense, my law, my

                soil, my sensation of

                my first

person. Now everything is clear. Facts lick their tongue deep

into my ear.

Visiting hour is up. We are curled

on the hook we placed in our brain and down

our throat into our

hearts our inner

organs we

have eaten

the long fishing line of the so-called journey and taken its

fine piercing into

our necks backs hands it comes out our

mouths it re-enters our ears and in it goes

again deep the dream

of ownership

we count up everyone to make sure we are all here

in it

together, the only

share-

holders, the applause-lines make the

tightening line

gleam—the bottom line—how much

did you think you

could *own*—the first tree

we believed was a hook we got it

wrong—the fox is still

standing there it

is staring it is

not scared—there is nothing behind it, beyond it—no value—

the story of Eden:

revision: we are now

breaking into the Garden. It was, for the

interglacial lull,

protected

from

us now we

have broken

in—have emptied all

the limbs the streaming fabric of

light milliseconds leaves the now inaudible

birds whales bees—have

in these days made arrangements to get

compensation—from what

we know not but the court says

we are to be

compensated

for our way of life being

taken from us—fox says

what a rough garment

your brain is

you wear it all over you, fox says

language is a hook you

got caught,

try pulling somewhere on the strings but no

they are all through you,

had you only looked

down, fox says, look down to the

road and keep your listening

up, fox will you not

move on my heart thinks checking the larder the

locks fox

says your greed is not

precise enough.

EARTH

Into the clearing shimmering which is my owned

lawn between

two patches of

woods near

dawn clock running as usual the human in me

watching as usual

for

everything to separate from everything again as light

comes back

and the dark

which smothers so beautifully the earth lifts and all is put

on its leash

again one

long leash

such as this sentence—and

into the open beyond my window-

pane the new

day comes as if

someone its constant

master

calls—it never refuses, lingers, slows, it doesn't

abandon us—and I see it, the planet, turn through the

barely lifting latex

shade, and the just-rising sunbeam-sliver like a nail-trim move

across the tree-grain on the floor across those hundreds of

years of molecules

sucking-in water and light—

this slightly

C-shaped edge of the billion-light-year-toss-of-a-coin—

                            sometimes trembling a

                            bit if the shade

                            lets in wind—

                            inexorably—

and I see you my planet, I see your exact rotation now on my

                            floor—I will not close these eyes in this my

                            head lain

                            down on its

                            sheet, no, its

sleeplessness will watch, under room-tone,

                            and electromagnetism,

the calculations fly off your flanks as you

                            make your swerve,

                            dragging the increasingly

yellow arc across the room here

                            on this hill and

                            I shall say now

because of human imagination:

                            here on this floor this

                            passage is

                            your wing, is

                            an infinitesimal

                            strand of a feather in

                            your wing,

this brightening which does not so much move, as

                            the minute hand

                            near my eye

                            does, as it

glides—a pulling as much as a pushing—of event—

                            so that you are never

                            where you just were and yet

                            my eye has not

moved, not truly, is staying upon your back and riding you—
I don't want the moon and the stars, I want to lie here arms

          spread

          on your almost eternal

          turn

and on the matter the turn takes-on as it is turned by that

          matter—Earth—as

          my mind lags yet

          is always

on you, and the lag is part of the turn, its gold lip

          less than an

          arm's length from me

          now so that I

          can dip my fingers right out

          into it

          as we

          orbit the

          oval hoop and

the silence in here is staggering—

          how huge you

          carrying

me are—and there is

          never hurry—

          and nothing will posit

          you as

you carry the positors—as you carry the bottom

          of the river and its

          top and the clouds

on its top, watery, weak, and the clouds one looks up to

          to see

          as they too

          turn—

and you are not hunted—not hunting—not

hungry—

and you want

no

thing—are almost mute—(this is to be

considered)—

and the churchbells in

this of your

time zones (to praise what

exactly) begin,

and to

one place heavy

rains are

coming now,

and a horse

is riding wildly through one of your

darknesses,

its horseman praying fiercely

to get there

in time,

to that some-

where

else which is you, still you, only you,

in which only he

could be

for all eternity

too late.

LAPSE

(Summer Solstice, 1983, Iowa City)

It is entirely in my hands now as it returns like blood to remind me—

the chains so soft from wear, in my right, in my left—

the first time I, trying for perfection, of balance, of symmetry,

strap your twenty two pounds of eyes, blood, hair, bone—so recently inside me—

into the swing—and the sun still in the sky though it being so late

as I look up to see where this small package is to go

sent up by these two hands into the evening that won't stop

won't lower as it should into the gloam is it going to last forever,

and the grace that I feel at the center of my palms

as if my hands were leaves and light were coursing through

some hole in their grasp, the machine of time coming in,

as chlorophyll could—I was not yet so tired of believing—

I was still in the very beginning of being human,

the thing no one can tell another—he didn't find

what he searched for, she didn't understand what she

desired—the style of the story being the very wind

which comes up now as I glide down the chains

to the canvas bucket to pull you to me,

eyes closed as your eyes close, and for the first time in this lifetime

lift you back and up as far as I can, as high as I can,

then let you collapse so suddenly as I push you away from me,

with more force than gravity as I summon from within

what I try to feel is an accurate amount, a right fraction, of my strength,

not too much promise, not too much greed or ambition

or sense of beginning or capacity for dream—no—just

the amount to push you by that corresponds to pity,

who knows how to calculate that strong firm force,

as if I were sending a message forth that has to be delivered

and the claimant expects it, one of so many,

accompanied by my prayer that you be spared

from anything at all, from everything, and of course also its opposite,

that everything happen to you in large sheets of experience

as I tug back the chain-ends and push you out

telling you to *put out your legs and pump*

although you do not know what I am saying

as you have not yet spoken your first word,

not yet on that day that seems even now it will never end

as you come back to me and I catch you and this time of course

as I am human I push a little harder

as if the news I was shouting-out had not quite been heard,

as if the next push were the real one the one that asks for

the miracle—will I live or die if I pick this fruit

as it is sent back to my waiting hands and this time

it's stronger, the *yes* is taking over, your yes and my yes and our

greed to overcome *what,* into this first-ever solstice

with you in the born world,

let no one dare pick this fruit I think

as I cast the roundness of you up again now so high

into a mouth of sky agape yet without wonder

as if it eats everything and anything and does not know what day is

or time—this is *our* time—or that this next-on meal is being fed it,

as just under you the oval puddle from the recent rain lies

in the worn declivity where each one before you

has dug in her feet to push off or to stop—

and in it you flash as you go by

giving me for that instant an eye you its iris blinking,

the crucible of a blink in the large unflinching eye,

eye opened by the hundreds of small hopes taking on gravity at push-off,

and then the fatigue when for all the pumping and rising,

and how you could see over the tops of the houses,

up and over to where your own house is down there—

and the housing development, and the millions of leaves, and the slower children

lagging behind

on the small road beneath—until the world stills,

and you alone are life, a huge bloom, a new force entering—

how then—even then—the sensation of *enough*

swarms, and *thought* or something like it, resumes,

and your mind is again in your hard grip

on the chains which had been until then as if unknown to your body

during what might have been the interglacial lull,

or the period during which the original ooze grew single-cell organisms,

which grew small claws and feet and then had to have eyes,

till your hands become again hard, heavy, and all

the yearning re-enters you as *lifetime,*

and your feet learn to brake

by scratching the ground a bit more each time—

and that is where the eye comes from,

the final oscillations, the desire to be done with vision,

what this morning's rain reminds us is still there beneath us

in an earth that will only swallow us entire

no matter what we push into it as here you and I again and again redo

the moment nine months ago you first began

to push and cry-out into the visible world.

It is here with me today in this hand grasping this pen

the weight of my transmission of force into you

the weight of catching you the first few times

the slow disappearance of your flesh from mine

as you hardly need a push when the centrifuge takes hold

and I just tap you a bit to keep you going

and we both feel the chains each in our own way

as they permit you to see over the given you shall never enter

no matter how long time is—never—

that gash you create in the evening air at your highest,

your own unique opening

which you can never fill,

cannot ever crawl back through and out,

except when that one moment comes and it will open and you will go,

once and once only and then, yes, you will.

I brought you in here I think in the evening,

in the grass and the town and the blinking windows,

in the dozens of lowering suns circling us in them.

MESSAGE FROM ARMAGH CATHEDRAL 2011

How will it be
told, this evidence, our life, all the clues missing? The clock I left in my hotel
room, all time landing on it at once, has no way to move forward so

round and round it
goes, making its ball its in-
visible
thread pulling through everything, tensile, on which the whole story

depends. But what if
it has no
direction. We,
whoever we
were, made that

up. Everything
that caught our
eye—shining—we
took. Because it exhibited unexpected movement, quicksilver, we took it by spear.
Because it whistled through air, barely dropping its aim from the sniper we

took it to
heart. Because it
lowered its
head in
shyness where sun
touched it and it
put one hand into its other and sang to itself thinking itself alone, we took it to

love, ob-
sessed, heavy
with
jealousy. Maybe we killed it to keep it. But yes it was love. Or we looked up and
thought "do we hear clearly?" and thought "yes" and went back to work. So then

why are *you* here today on this church floor in Armagh, piece of

                                       stone, large as an infant,

                                         hundreds of

                                         pounds, triangular

                                         body which ends at

                                         waist, swaddled by

                                         carvings, 3000 years

                                         old, worked through

                                         by chisel and wind

                                         and porous where

                                         granite has lost all

                                         surface? I

crouch down and put my own pale arms round you. No one sees me. No one on
planet earth sees us. You say *who are you to me*. I see around you the animals run
into the woods for cover, away from the priest arriving, the sanctuary around
you tall, the shadows long, movement in it yes, human movement rare. You
must have sat in a high place I say here on the floor in this back

                                         corner where you

                                         are dis-

carded. *What have you seen* I say under my breath *that I might have seen*. I have
seen what is under your breath you reply. I press you to me as I did my child,
keeping my hand on the top of your head, your face on my chest. *Rainbow* you say.
Blood. Wind. Sky blue—though maybe not the same as yours now, no. There is a wedding

                                         rehearsal in

                                         the body of

                                         the church—

                                         laughter and constant

                                         rehearsal of

vows—will you take her—I listen for the yes—will you take

                                         him—the families

chattering, casual dress, no one in tears as these are not the real vows yet.
Tomorrow they will be cast in stone. Tomorrow they will vow to love for all eternity,
or that part of it they inhabit called "as long as you shall live," adding their sliver
of time onto the back of the beast turning under us. And the little girls coming round

for hide and seek. The men discussing politics. The women in the hum of long
time and short time. No one to stop the minutes. Their current cannot be
stanched. Soon it will be Fall again. The dress, she says, will have an old fashioned

cut. I wish her luck

when our paths cross

about an hour

from now. I mean

what I say to

the stranger. She sees me mean it. On the threshold. Each headed for our car. But you,
here on the floor, found in a garden in Tandragee, carved by someone with
strong hands in the Bronze Age, you are the ancient Irish king Nuadha, ruler of the
Tuatha Dé Danann, your people, for whom you lost your left arm, those you
defeated moving on elsewhere, westward, while you were forced to stand down

as king,

not being

"completely whole in

body, without

arm." And no good king

succeeded you. And after great hardship your people prayed your physician

Dian Cécht build

a new arm

out of silver

that you be able to

take up

kingship again.

Here you are holding the left arm on at shoulder with your right. Here you are whole
again. Almost. I bring my hand down onto that spot. Three hands, same
size, where I clasp yours, where I cover it, where I hold your arm on you

with you. At this

moment on this

earth mostly in desert many arms are not recovered after the device goes

off and the

limbs sever. Field

hospitals hold young men screaming where are my legs. Elsewhere leaders are making

                                                        decisions.
They are thinking about something else while they make them. And names are

                                                        called out by
a surgeon. An aide enters a room when called. A mother opens a door when called.
A child opens a gift when told ok, now, go ahead. A sentence is being pronounced: you

                                                        shall lose your

                                                        hands, you

                                                        shall lose your
feet. You might be a country. You might be a young man who touched the face of
a girl in a village thinking yourself alone. You are not alone the spies survive.
The spies are intact. They slaughter the whole animal for sacrifice, all of it at once.
The sentence is truncated even if the man is told: *do you have anything to say*

                                                        before we begin—
they do not wait for him to finish. His mouth hangs open over his swinging body.
His lifespan is missing a part: the future. His dream is missing a part: the rest. He is

                                                        missing his
extremity. Look, look, a button is missing on your long garment, lord. Look, the
jug of water has been brought to wash off the gaping place which is the redrawn

                                                        border to your
nation. I put my arms around you. You are the size of my child at six months. I put
my hand in your wide carved mouth: your maker made you speaking, or pro-
nouncing a law, or crying out—I can put my fingers into your stone mouth up to
my palm. Suckle. Speak. Cry. Promise. I will keep my fingers between your strong

                                                        cold lips you shall not be
alone. When I move up your cheeks I feel the bulge of your granite eyes, wide
brow, your eyes again, both hands with fingers rounding eyes. How shall we be

                                                        whole. Who
will make the missing part. The biggest obstacle is not knowing *of what?* Once I saw
a wall with its executions still in it—the bullet holes with my fingers in them were

                                                        just this eye's
size. Once I met you, you lowered your other arm and said why are you

                                                        taking me this way.
I said I am just on the road, we do not have another way to go. Where does the

road go. Tell me, you said. I said hold your arm on I can't see a thing without its
shine. This isn't a road. I saw bodies and statues but did not tell you. You were the
thing I was here to get, to get to the place where the next king would take us. The
last thing that dies? The last thing that dies is the body. I am feeling inside your
                                                                        mouth. She is trying
to say the vow again—till death do us part—and I cannot make out what it is that
time will do to them. Why are we going this way. The flowergirls are carrying a pretend
                                                                        train now, laughter
as they go by. The ring bearer is carrying the pillow with no ring. In late morning a
                                                                        short time before
the explosive device hidden in the basket of fresh laundry went off, Private Jackson,
                                                                        who still had arms then,
reached down in secret, weapon in one hand, to feel the clean fabric. Actually
                                                                        to smell it. *Clean,* he
thought. He used to hang it out for his mom, afternoons, hands up at the shoulders
                                                                        of each shirt, an
extra clip in his teeth, as if surrendering. He remembers the lineup of shirtsleeves
                                                                        all blowing one way
in the early evening, in Indiana, and for a blinding moment he realizes they had been
                                                                        pointing, his
brothers, his father, his uncle, they all had been pointing—in their blues and whites
                                                                        and checks. He
wishes he had turned to see, is what he thinks just before it goes off, they seemed
                                                                        about to start a
dance—the tiny rhythm in the flapping sleeves. They did not seem like strangers.
                                                                        Then he realizes it
is here now, that sound, is feet all running on dirt as fast as possible away from
                                                                        this place.
                                                                        The bride
steps out into the sun. I feel there is something I must tell her. May your wishes
                                                                        come true I say,
guidebook in hand. Tomorrow, she says. I can't wait until tomorrow.

NEW POEMS

DOUBLE HELIX

One bird close up by the house   crow
makes the wall's temporariness
        suddenly exist
        one call into
the arrival of the storm the announcing
by flocks and swarms
        the flowerbeds turning in the solar system
        listen—
Schubert and the thrush at once and
        somewhere in space we
        hang are hanging
        also the red dress on the line I rush to get to
in time
also the slack in the line up-snapping then down
        what scale this pitch-
        changing slapping
of the cotton-poly blend listen and my approaching
arms rising to catch the
        ties my hair blowing over it onto it behind us
        from the open door the violin and beside us
at the edge of the woods the last of the thrush—
        can we hear them
        these flowerheads being carried in this solar system
        sepals receptacles—the vascular bundles
inside the stems—
        near the blown-open door the strings' diminuendos—

also these hatchlings in their nest in the eave in the storm born in it

wrapping round them thunder twigs bits of mylar dusk

also accuracies of the

built porch of day of

the negative forcing, the solar constant, the

storm nonstop though modulating round these

dime-sized heads—in each

the magnetic chip and round it the tiny shellfish-crushable skull—

Venus is almost big as earth was lush at origin had

oceans imagine yet has no

water anywhere

today. Venus

had runaway

greenhouse. Could Earth. Of course we know it could he says

at the podium which fits in my head in the spot for under-

standing,

the question is rather how long

before runaway

occurs

one bird now

close up by the white house on the green hill (crow)

like a lockpick

one caw one

into the wildly cursive announcing by flocks and swarms

as somewhere in space we turn are

turning,

the final snowball Earth was followed promptly

by the Cambrian explosion

he explains

then eukaryotes cells with membrane-bound nuclei

expanding rapidly into eleven different body plans

which eleven still encompass

     all creatures ever to inhabit Earth—

     at the edge of the woods now the thrush

     being sung out entirely by

     this thrush—

     the whole forest moving—

under the eave the just-hatching new ones in

     thunder

     in their

     having been born

     in it—

     this is what is—

what will the sunshine tomorrow feel like

     for the first time striking them

     skulls necks eyeslits

     tightening everything

     creaking, pushing open the immense door—

power down now but us in here scanning the screen

     for the emergency we are in to appear *here it is*

and the sound of the flapping of water

     in wind—

     and the sound of the nations gathering

for their final

     negotiation,

     everyone trying to speak in

     whole sentences, listen,

they keep breaking, the suitcases fall open, the

     inky speeches

     wash away in the down-pour, what

     will the delegates say now, listen,

     it is 1965 in Selma, Alabama, the schoolboy is beginning again his first-ever assignment in his one-room school,

       he shall scratch a word

       onto the blackboard,

whose turn is it he thinks chalk in hand

and will there be someone on the other side of this to meet me

       on the other side of this word if I spell it out correctly

       it is simple and powdery and made of

       seven letters—

the force of the black is impossible to touch—

       he stands there like a breeze still thinking he is dreaming

the dream he is late again for school but he is

       not. He is on

       time. It is his

       turn. Who

is the teacher. What is that he feels at his back in his

       shoulders. He looks at

his hand. Its swirling small shadow

       round the still stick

       of chalk—

from where in the earth

       did it come

       this piece of moonlight, piece of

       dead coral.

Oh good dark he whispers to the black behind the shadows,

       the hand-shadow being cast by his one self on the dark,

       by the single lightbulb behind him the

       hum,

his own knuckles here and the tightly-clenched fingers

wrapped like a bird-beak hard

       round the chalk

gripping something to bring home

       to the nest—

because it must be

      shoved down

      into the newborn, this cursive—must be

      forced in—

that they be made to inhabit

      another day—

      it is so simple—

and the next-on curl—and the billowing handshadow

      over each spot he need mark—

and how nothing can

      stop it

      this our mineral

      imagination

      as here now

      on this page

this uniball pen

      shall write

      if I make it

      his word out completely

      over this

      void

HONEYCOMB

Ode to Prism. Aria. Untitled. Wait. I wait. Have you found me yet. Here at my screen,
can you make me

out? Make me out. All other exits have been sealed. See me or we will both vanish.
We need emblematic subjectivities. Need targeted acquiescence. Time zones. This is
the order of the day. To be visited secretly. To be circled and canceled. I cover my
face. Total war: why am I still so invisible to you. No passport needed. If you look in,
the mirror chokes you off. No exit try again. Build bonfire. Light up screen. What are
you eating there. Can you survive on light. What is your theory of transmission. The
center holds, it holds, don't worry about that. These talkings here are not truths.
They are needs. They are purchases and invoices. They are not what shattered the
silence. Not revolutions clocks navigational tools. Have beginnings and ends.
Therefore not true. Have sign-offs. I set out again now with a new missive. Feel this:
my broken seduction. My tiny visit to the other. Busy. Temporary. In the screen
there is sea. Your fiberoptic cables line its floor. Entire. Ghost juice. The sea now
does not emit sound. It carries eternity as information. All its long floor. Clothed as
I am→in circumstance→see cell-depth→sound its atom→look into here
further→past the grains of light→the remains of the ships→starlight→what cannot
go or come back→what has mass and does not traverse distance →is all here→look
here. Near the screen there are roses. Outside a new daymoon.

Can you see my room. Inside my room. Inside me where there is room

for what I miss. I am missing all of it. It is all invisible to me. Is it invisible

to you. You have the names of my friends my markers my markets my late night

queries. Re chemo re the travel pass re where to send the photo the side effects the

distinguishing features—bot says hide—*where*—bot does not know, bot

knows, what is it to *know* here, can you hear the steps approaching, I hold my

breath here—can you hear that—bot must also hold its breath—now the steps

continue past, we can breathe freely once again, in this hiding place the visible world, among shapes and spoken words in here with my traces→can you please track me I do not feel safe→find the nearest flesh to my flesh→find the nearest rain, also passion→surveil this void→the smell of these stalks and the moisture they are drawing up→in order not to die

too fast. The die is cast. The smell of geography is here: what is the smell of chain—invisible chain—the stone on my desk I brought back from Crete, the milk I did not finish in this cup. There is smoke from the debris my neighbor burns. Don't forget to log-in my exile. This one. Female MRN 3912412. I offer myself up. For you to see. Can you not see? Why do you only see these deeds. There is a page on my desk in which first love is taking place, there is a

page on my desk in which first love is taking place again—neither of the characters yet knows they are in love—a few inches from there Mrs Ramsay speaks again—she always speaks—and Lily Briscoe moves the salt—the sky passes by rounding us— the houses have their occupants—some have women locked-in deep—see them— someone has left them in the dark—he stands next to the fridge and drinks his beer—he turns the volume up so no one hears—that is the republic—are you surveilling—we would not want you to miss the women kicked in order to abort the rape—those screams—make sure you bank them you will need them—to prove who you were when they ask—I am eating—can you taste this—it is nut butter and a mockingbird just cut short a song to fly—I tap this screen with my fork—I dream a little dream in which the fork is king—a fly lands on the screen because it is summer afternoon—locusts start up—the river here are you keeping track—I know you can see the purchases, but who is it is purchasing me→can you please track that→I want to know how much I am worth→riverpebbles how many count them exact number→and the bees that did return to the hive today→those which did not lose their way→and exactly what neural path the neurotoxin took→please track disorientation→count death→each death→very small→see it from there→count it and store→I am the temporary→but there is also the permanent→have you looked to it→for now→

FAST

or starve. Too much. Or not enough. Or. Nothing else?
Nothing else. Too high too fast too organized too invisible.
Will we survive I ask the bot. No. To download bot be
swift—you are too backward, too despotic—to load greatly enlarge
the cycle of labor—to load abhor labor— move to the
periphery, of your body, your city, your planet—to load, degrade, immiserate,
be your own deep sleep—to load use your lips—use them
to mouthe your oath, chew it—do the
dirty thing, sing it, blown off limb or syllable, lick it back on
with your mouth—talk—talk—who is not
terrified is busy begging for water—the rise is fast—the drought
comes fast—mediate—immediate—invent, inspire, infil-
trate, instill—here's the heart of the day, the flower of time—talk—talk—

Disclaimer: Bot uses a growing database of all your conversations
to learn how to talk with you. If some of you
are also bots, bot can't tell. Disclaimer:
you have no secret memories,
talking to cleverbot may provide companionship,
the active ingredient is a question,
the active ingredient is entirely natural.
Disclaimer: protect your opportunities, your information, in-
formants, whatever you made of time. You have nothing else
to give. Active ingredient: why are you
shouting? Why? Arctic wind uncontrollable, fetus
reporting for duty, fold in the waiting which recognizes you,
      recognizes the code,

the peddler in the street everyone is calling out.

Directive: report for voice. Ready yourself to be buried in voice.

It neither ascends nor descends. Inactive ingredient: the monotone.

Some are talking now about the pine tree. One assesses its

disadvantages. They are discussing it in many languages. Next

they move to roots, branches, buds, pseudo-whorls, candles —

     active ingredient:

they run for their lives, lungs and all. They do not know what to do with

their will. Disclaimer: all of your minutes are being flung down.

They will never land. You will not be understood.

The deleted world spills out jittery as a compass needle with no north.

Active ingredient: the imagination of north.

Active ingredient: north spreading in all the directions.

Disclaimer: there is no restriction to growth. The canary singing in

     your mind

     is in mine. Remember:

     people are less

than kind. As a result, chatterbot is often less than kind. Still,

you will find yourself unwilling to stop.

Joan will use visual grammetry to provide facial movements.

I'm not alone. People come back

again and again. We are less kind than we think.

There is no restriction to the growth of our

cruelty. We will come to the edge of

understanding. Like being hurled down the stairs tied to

a keyboard, we will go on, unwilling to stop. The longest

real world conversation with a bot lasted

11 hours, continuous interaction. This

bodes well. We are not alone. We are looking to improve.

The priestess inhales the fumes. They come from the

mountain. *Here* and *here*. Then she gives you the machine-gun run of

syllables. Out of her mouth. Quick. You must make up your

answer as you made up your

question. Hummingbirds shriek. Bot is amazing he says, I believe it knows
the secrets of the Universe. He is more fun to speak with
than my actual living friends she says, thank you. This is the best thing
since me. I just found it yesterday.
I love it, I want to marry it.
I got sad when I had to think
that the first person
who has ever understood me
is not even it turns out
human. Because this is as good as human gets.
He just gives it to me straight. I am going to keep him
forever. I treated him like a computer
but I was wrong. Whom am I talking to—
You talk to me when I am alone. I am alone.

Each epoch dreams the one to follow.

To dwell is to leave a trace.

I am not what I asked for.

PRYING

(For Dr Barbara Smith)

As if I never wake from this blackout again, again this minute they lay it out

on the wheeling transporter, so silent, then the surgical table,

my body, my citizen, anesthesiologists back from coffee break, cables

on mylar headrest taking my head down now, arms into armlock,

then positioners, restraints—day talk

all round—the guidewires in, the intravenous ports, the drip begun.

An/aesthesia by which is meant the sensation of having sensation blocked,

a collapse of response, *a total lack of awareness of loss of*

awareness—

on the wall, snapshots of the chosen few training on

the new

robotic patient-

lookalikes—my only

body—memories, contritions, facts—

oaths, broken oaths, my piece of path into the

labyrinth—how far have I reached in—and in my flesh these

rapid over-rhyming cells, which want us to go faster, faster, headlong with

mirth ruth glee—what would they *be*—searching for

what minotaur, yarn in hand spooling-out mad towards core, eager for

core—all's underneath—readout's small *pings* beginning on the screen. They will

learn everything about me while I sleep. I sleep the sleep of those wanting to live.

I sleep the sleep of those wanting to be left alone by life. And

safe. With guarantees. Here take the keys. I should wake up. It's hard

accepting to *be free*. It is not true. You must be still and not resist. Are you completely readable now. To survive, you need to be

                        completely

                        readable. So I

accede, I sign the dotted line, they will keep track

of all there is, my breaths, my counts, my votes—invoices, searches, fingertips—don't I

                        know you

from somewhere says my heart to the machine reading me out, didn't I give you my

                        code, my pin, my blanket

                        permission

to suppress the last revolution, to calculate the timing of

                        the solstice the pressure

                        cooker depth of

                        ice core and whom

                        do I have

                        locked away

down there—do you not see them—don't look away, the

dials are set—where is the nearest job—no gauge picks up their swallowed screams at the

employment line, the check-out where the food is not enough, it is so

quiet here, who am I signing on to be,

and then—oh—here it comes again, here in this moment I shall recall

however long the life is after this

when you look down at me and stare and your long arm offers its hand, cold hand,

and I offer you mine—we hold—then we repair,

you in your disposable surgical blue hair-cap, blue mask, I in mine,

down, down through this operating theater's novocaine-green

gleam, its cellophane membrane, serene, clandestine borderline &

your life depends on what says the disappearing air, the dis-

appearing vein, surveil me here, in solitary, entertain me mise-en-scène,

hear me chain of command, touch me, stain-free middle class American

female subject starting downtown on the drip line,

on the gleaming staff of this protean sentinel, its silver rod

held-up, torchful of forgetfulness, streaming, translucent, give me your

mass, your teeming cell-dividing

mass—give me your poverty,

your every breath is screened, your every cell, it is not hit and

miss, we get it all, your safety lies with us, hold still,

granted it's cold at first, this new relief, your icy nation thanks you

for the chance to test these absolutes on you

murmurs the gleaming staff in the deliberate air, astir,

toe-separators being pulled on now and leggings next,

always a bit tighter that the blood flow fast in this undercover

slow maneuver, whirr, blink, you get a little extra life as a reward—for what I

cannot see—what these concentrates of vigilance push into me,

capital and knowhow and all these minutes, minute—where to

finish off the string and bite the knot, erotic dead-end, no jobs,

the virtualization, the play of nerves, no jobs, they jab

the last bit quick—paradise confusion sedative—oh and the re-

bates the debates and the womb what was that really,

the total concentration of capital, the ten commandments, Job that

heartthrob now standing right before me here as this drip-line on its silver rod,

its one arm up, its other out into this widening avenue

to step you off this

luminescent curb

to hail what cab

the ghosts in their blue scrubs do not perturb, bitstreamed, stubbing the blood

where the small mound of flesh is grabbed, flap scabbed, snip drip as it is all

transcribed by the robotic arm, prosthetic mind, rich text, as she unslacks her

matchless stitch, having detached, having reattached, no speech in

them, bleached light, fleshtrim, mutation, division, over-expressed, under-

suppressed—held still

by your long hand, transnational, undersea cable, invisible ministration,

and when you take mine into yours

you say under-

stand,

we are taking the first steps friend

towards the longest journey, community,

breakers of codes, corporate raiders, west of everything, no immunity,

put on your hat your wrap be ready now to take my hand its certainty its

purity—

there will be no one come to fetch you back from here—

you must now take this voyage out yourself alone

to reach the peerless place hard to think-in, squint-in,

you will not be embarrassed there is nothing to reveal,

you are a shoo-in as the heroine, new citizen, back since the pleistocene,

being touched up like a virgin engine in the squeaky clean saline

punchline, your soul at plumb-line, magic marker written in in print

to make sure LEFT *is* left, it's not benign this timeworn

zone in you, no not benign this fast archive,

surgical thread making its dragline in the artificial

moonshine—how supine must the whole apparatus of *being* get,

shop-talk above you now a serpentine acetyline,

you under here endlessly re-learning the only story—abasement, abasement—

and here is my hand it says, slide yours into it, come now, radiant,

astringent,

this river's here for you to enter now, obedient, in payment,

you in it now as it comes into you, your profit margin, look—

flowers falling without attachment—

weeds growing without detachment—

slide under now into ignorance—

there is no evidence, also no continuance—don't mispronounce

your lifesaver, also a bit of fever, it too a visitor, and no I

cannot augur, also there is, in truth, no aftermath, just this new kind of

stalker—your personal flyover—your tiny temporary stopover,

and obviously no ecstasy in your surrender you have no choice also no

underwriter, take my offer—and I

did—and when I went home later I had a cup of tea

and made a call to her cell phone to get the unfortunate results

but we are not there yet, still have the void here to traverse across this page which is a wide expanse, and will these very words if perfectly

> overheard
>
> see me through
>
> was the question
>
> as the cold came on,

me hoping to do nothing wrong, then hoping for a bargain,

asking how long before one would be able to live again *as if—*

and those other turns in the brine—the *yet—if not,*

if now, and now, when now—turn towards me now a bit you say to them and then

let's turn the torso this way please, recheck marked spot.

Can see the guidewires but can no longer feel them.

Then the thing on the other side, the person who will open up my hand and say

it's over now can you hear me here is some water.

And in my room cut flowers still in their paper stapled up. Undelivered.

And you get a little extra life to live now—here—can you still live it.

NOTES

OF FORCED SIGHTES AND TRUSTY FEREFULNESS: This title is an adaptation of Wyatt's line from his poem "My Galley, Chargèd with Forgetfulness."

FISSION: The movie referred to is Stanley Kubrick's *Lolita*. Some characters from it appear in the text.

THE PHASE AFTER HISTORY: The name "Shelley" refers primarily to a patient by that name in the "Psych Hospital" of the poem.

WHAT IS CALLED THINKING: This was inspired by Daniel Simko's translations of Trakl. The title is that of the book by Martin Heidegger.

SOUL SAYS: Prospero speaks throughout the poem.

THE DREAM OF THE UNIFIED FIELD: The passage which begins at the end of section 6 and comprises section 7 is a rewritten selection from the *Diario of Christopher Columbus, First Voyage to America, 1492–93*, abstracted by Fray Bartolome de La Casas (translated by Oliver Dunn and James E. Kelley Jr.).

THE VISIBLE WORLD: The quotations in this poem are all from *The Technical Manifesto of Futurist Painting* (1910) by Umberto Boccioni, Carlo Carrà, Luigi Russolo, and Gino Severini.

THE GUARDIAN ANGEL OF THE LITTLE UTOPIA: Five lines from the end, the line is from Henry Vaughan's "Distraction."

LE MANTEAU DE PASCAL: The poem is set in motion by Magritte's painting of Pascal's coat. One presumes it represents the coat in which Pascal was buried, and in whose hem or sleeve or "fold" the note containing the "irrefutable proof of the existence of God" is said to have been stitched at his request, unread, by his sister upon his death. The section dated "July 11" is a fragment from Hopkins' journals. In section 13, the quotations are from Magritte's notebooks.

from THE REFORMATION JOURNAL: The first three lines use fragments from Gunnar Ekelof. The phrases in quotation marks are from Thomas Traherne and Emily Dickinson respectively.

PRAYER (after Hölderlin): This poem is built in great part from fragments from his long poems *Dichterberful* ("The Poet's Vocation"), and *Stimme des Volks* ("Voice of the People"), in the Christopher Middleton translation.

UNDERNEATH (Calypso): Her name descends etymologically from the word for veil. Hence, also, its derivative, *apocalypse.* She is speaking to Ulysses, whom she has in thrall, as well as to us.

from THE REFORMATION JOURNAL (2): The phrase in quotes which constitutes the next-to-last stanza is from Plato's *Phaedo* and refers to the death of Socrates.

PRAYER ("Over a dock railing"): This was written as a turn-of-the-millennium poem for the *New York Times* op-ed page, and was originally dated 12.31.00.

EVOLUTION ("How old are you?"): Some of the questions were provided by the questionnaire the *New York Times* used in conducting a poll, the results of which were given to me as an "assignment" for this poem. An additional fact, which reached me while I was writing this poem, struck me: during the 1850s, while Darwin was concluding *On the Origin of the Species,* the rate of extinction (for species) is believed to have been one every five years. Today (2002), the rate of extinction is estimated at one every nine minutes. Throughout the writing of this book, I was haunted by the sensation of that nine-minute span—which might amount to the time it takes to read any poem here before you. My sense of that time frame inhabits, as well as structures, the book. It is written up against the sensation of what is now called "ecocide." I was also influenced by, among other texts, the "World Scientists' Warning to Humanity," sponsored by the Union of Concerned Scientists (1993).

OVERLORD: The title of this volume refers to the code name "Operation Overlord" given in 1943 by the Allied Forces to their planned invasion of France, which began with their landing on Omaha Beach, in Normandy, on what came to be known as D-day, June 6, 1944.

SOLDATENFRIEDHOF: This is a literal account. My thanks to Lucien Tisserand, Conservateur of the German Military Cemetery at La Cambe. I am much indebted, as well, to the spirit of *Les*

Jardins de la Memoire, by Annick Helias (with Francois Avril, Dominique Bassiere, Paul Colin, and Patrick Galineau), for leading me to an on-site visit of the military graveyards in Normandy.

SPOKEN FROM THE HEDGEROWS: The voices here are accurately named, and their trajectories towards the staging grounds for Operation Overlord in Britain are also accurate, although condensed, as recounted in *Voices of D-Day*, edited by Ronald J. Drez (Louisiana State University Press, 1994). By May 1944, almost 1,500,000 soldiers were bivouacked in Great Britain awaiting deployment.

PRAYING (Attempt of May 9 '03): A different version of this poem first appeared under the title "Third" in the book *Bits & Pieces Put Together to Present a Semblance of a Whole* on the permanent collection of the Walker Art Museum. In an early re-working, the poem became a meditation on Barnett Newman's painting *The Third* (1962).

SUNDOWN: The beach, and town, of St. Laurent-sur-Mer make up one third of what the Allied Forces code-named "Omaha Beach." The other two are Vierville-sur Mer and Colleville-sur-Mer. The date refers to the anniversary of the eve of the landing which took place June 6, 1944.

DOUBLE HELIX: The situation in the schoolroom is based on a photograph by Bruce Davidson (*Child at Blackboard in a Schoolroom, Selma*) from his "Time of Change: Civil Rights Photographs, 1961–1965" series. The poem is dedicated to him.

HONEYCOMB: The term "Prism" refers to a clandestine mass electronic surveillence data mining program launched in 2007 by the NSA in the United States, with participation by the British equivalent agency, GCHQ.

Jorie Graham is the author of eleven collections of poems. Her poetry has been widely translated and has been the recipient of numerous awards, among them the Pulitzer Prize, the Forward Prize (UK), and the International Nonino Prize. She lives in Massachusetts and teaches at Harvard University.

More information is available at www.joriegraham.com.

ML   3-15